Holiness for Everyone

Eric Sammons

Holiness for Everyone

The Practical Spirituality of
St. Josemaría Escrivá

SOPHIA INSTITUTE PRESS
Manchester, New Hampshire

For Fr. Scott Woods, who first convinced
me that holiness was truly possible.

Contents

A Note on the Major Works of St. Josemaría Escrivá viii

Foreword ix

Introduction. 3

Part One
Laying the Foundation

1. Called to Be Saints. 9
2. A Modern-Day Saint 21
3. Abba! Father! 33
4. Free to Love 51
5. Ambitious for Holiness 65

Part Two
Building a Saintly Life

6. Be a Contemplative in the Midst of the World. 81
7. Make Your Work a Way to Heaven 99
8. Live in the Family of God 115
9. Proclaim Christ to the World. 127

Conclusion. 141

Acknowledgments 145

About the Author. 147

A Note on the Major Works of
St. Josemaría Escrivá

The following works of St. Josemaría Escrivá are cited throughout the book. In keeping with standard convention, they are referenced by point number, not page number.

The Way
The Forge
Furrow
Christ Is Passing By
Friends of God
Conversations with Josemaría Escrivá
In Love with the Church
The Way of the Cross
Holy Rosary

Foreword

Life has taught me that a family is not simply a household and its inhabitants. My wife, Kimberly, and I have watched our children grow; and now they've begun to marry and have children of their own, make homes of their own. Each of their homes has a style all its own, though I'm pleased to recognize so many of the customs they received from their mom and dad.

A family, when it's functional, is really a family of families — each constituent group a little different from all the others, but all holding on to some common inheritance. It makes for rollicking conversation at holidays and reunions. It makes for unforgettable holidays and vacations.

The Church, too, is a family of families. We have dioceses and parishes, movements and religious orders, eastern rites and western, sodalities, and even military orders — each a little different from the others, but all holding on to the same apostolic tradition, all of them Catholic.

My family within the family is called Opus Dei (Latin for "The Work of God"), which was founded by St. Josemaría Escrivá in 1928. The teachings of that saint are the subject of this wonderful book by Eric Sammons. I myself have written a book about "The Work." It's titled *Ordinary Work, Extraordinary Grace: My Journey in Opus Dei,* and it's a personal account, an insider's view, though addressed to anyone who might be interested or curious.

I could not have written a book like Eric's. Perhaps I could not have written a book as useful as Eric's, for he sees my family inheritance from a different perspective. He is not a member of Opus Dei—though he has studied its spirit and learned from it—and so he sees it from the outside. Sometimes that means he sees it more clearly and more attentively and more appreciatively. He has helped me to gain a better appreciation for the family life to which God has called me.

Eric knows that the heart of family life is the parent-child bond. In natural families, that heart is not always healthy. In no natural family is it perfect. But the heart of Opus Dei is something greater. Opus Dei draws its life from the fact of divine filiation—the fact that all Christians become children of God through baptism. That doctrine took hold of St. Josemaría Escrivá as God inspired him to spell out what it means for children of God to live in a material world.

Yet the idea was not original with St. Josemaría, and it is not the private property of Opus Dei. It is the common tradition of the Catholic Church. In the Catholic view, we are not merely saved from something, but for something. We are saved from sin, but for sonship. So freed, we may enjoy "the glorious liberty of the children of God" (Rom. 8:21). St. Paul wrote: "All who are led by the Spirit of God are sons of God. For you did not receive the spirit of slavery to fall back into fear, but you have received the spirit of sonship. When we cry 'Abba! Father!' it is the Spirit himself bearing witness with our spirit that we are children of God" (Rom. 8:14–16).

> "See what love the Father has given us, that we should be called children of God; and so we are. . . . Beloved, we are God's children now" (1 John 3:1–2).

Our share in Christ's sonship is not our work, but the work of God. It is the essence of our salvation as well as the defining feature of Opus Dei.

Eric Sammons shows that St. Josemaría has recovered the most powerful truth of classic Christianity and restated it in a way that is compelling for men and women (and children) of our time.

And since he has been canonized a saint, his teaching now belongs not only to his "family within the family," but to the great family. Opus Dei—as a way of sanctification in the world, a way to sanctify our ordinary work—belongs to the Church, belongs to everybody.

—*Scott Hahn*

Holiness for Everyone

Introduction

What is your goal in life?

When I was a kid, I wanted to be a baseball player, a fireman, and a super-hero. As I got older, my goals became more modest: have a happy family and be able to provide for them. Such goals are not uncommon today.

What is God's goal for your life?

It might surprise you to know that God's goal for you is nothing less than sainthood. St. Paul wrote, "For this is the will of God, your sanctification" (1 Thess. 4:3). And what is "sanctification"? It is the perfecting of our minds and wills so that they are more and more like God's. In other words, God wants us to be like Him! This becoming more and more Godlike is what saints such as St. Francis of Assisi and St. Thérèse of Lisieux did in their lives, and it is what God wants — and expects — from each of us.

But how do we become a saint, especially in the modern world, which constantly pushes us away from sanctity? Fortunately for us, there was a twentieth-century priest who was devoted to answering this question — and we should listen to him, for he was canonized a saint. Who is this priest and saint? Josemaría Escrivá, the founder of Opus Dei.

I am always intrigued by the mysterious aura that surrounds this modern saint. Although Opus Dei numbers only around ninety-five thousand members (out of two billion Catholics), its reputation is outsized. And its mystique predates Dan Brown. Even before the popular author made an Opus Dei albino monk-assassin a main character in his blockbuster *The DaVinci Code* (in spite of the fact that there are no monks in Opus Dei, and presumably no assassins … at least not unrepentant ones), many rank and file Catholics already viewed Opus Dei—and by extension, St. Josemaría—with suspicion. Not since the early days of the Jesuits had a Catholic organization stirred up such mystery. Brown's book augmented this aura and popularized it.

Fortunately, a number of books in recent years have done much to clarify the work of Opus Dei. John Allen's Opus Dei gives an objective overview of the organization and its history. Scott Hahn, a member of the group, gives a worthwhile personal look at his own path in it in his book *Ordinary Work, Extraordinary Grace*. And, of course, there are many books published by Opus Dei itself, usually directed toward the group's own members, that explain the purpose of the organization.

This, however, is not a book about Opus Dei, nor is it directed toward members of the organization—though I hope they, too, benefit from it. I am not a member of Opus Dei, although I have participated in a number of its spiritual activities. The intention of this book is to spread the message of St. Josemaría on becoming a saint beyond the boundaries of Opus Dei.

When Catholics hear mention of St. Josemaría, too many think, "Oh, he's the Opus Dei saint," and then relegate his life and teachings as applicable only to Opus Dei members. What a shame. As you will see in these pages, St. Josemaría developed over many years of work and prayer among laypeople a spirituality whose goal is the sanctity of every man and woman. He insisted that every person could, with the grace of God, achieve holiness through ordinary life and work. In other words, he did not intend his spirituality only for an elite group, or for those separate from the world, or for a select subset of laypeople. He intended it for all people, no matter their state in life.

As any member of Opus Dei will tell you, joining its ranks is a vocation, a call from God. It is not for everyone. Furthermore, because of Opus Dei's relatively small size, its outreach is not available to everyone. But the spirituality of St. Josemaría is for everyone—laborer, executive, mother, teacher. Regardless of your state in life, the teachings of St. Josemaría can help you draw closer to God in ordinary life and grow in holiness. In this book I hope to make St. Josemaría's teachings accessible to non-Opus Dei members so that they can benefit from them just as so many members of the apostolate he founded have for decades. St. Josemaría is a canonized saint of the entire Catholic Church, not just one segment of it.

Our first step toward understanding St. Josemaría's message will be understanding the traditional Catholic teaching, forgotten at times, but renewed in recent years, of the call that each and every Christian has to holiness. St. Josemaría's spirituality did not develop in a vacuum, but instead stands on the shoulders of the entire tradition of Catholic spirituality. Yet he did bring something new to the Church, a way of approaching holiness that fits perfectly with the modern world. As the saint liked to say, his message was "as old and as new as the Gospel."[1] Next, we will examine the life of this extraordinary saint, that we might know the man whose spirituality seeks to sanctify our lives. Then—and before moving on to the practical advice St. Josemaría has for us—we will delve

---

[1] Josemaría Escrivá, *Conversations with Saint Josemaria Escriva* (New York: Scepter Publishers, 2008), 24. Available at Escriva Works, https://www.escrivaworks.org/book/conversations-contents.htm.

into the foundational principles of St. Josemaría's spirituality: our calling as children of God through Jesus Christ; our freedom as persons ransomed by Christ's saving work; and the "holy ambition," or driving desire for holiness, that should be the hallmark of a believer striving for Heaven.

St. Josemaría wove each of these three principles into his entire spirituality of sanctity through ordinary life. But his was not a theoretical spirituality, more comfortable in ivory towers than the streets and homes of regular Catholics. No, St. Josemaría developed a practical spirituality that gives concrete means for ordinary people to achieve holiness in the midst of their duties and responsibilities. Specifically, I divide his practical advice into three areas of life: the life of prayer; professional work, which we will see includes all the activities of life; and life within the Church. By applying the spirituality of St. Josemaría to each of these areas, we draw closer to God—not by joining a monastery, but by sanctifying the very life we are now living. And, of course, the Christian life is not self-focused: St. Josemaría also emphasized the importance of sharing the faith with others—carrying out an apostolate in the world that is a natural outgrowth of our daily walk with God.

As we will see, St. Josemaría developed a practical means for any person—no matter his vocation—to strive for holiness in the midst of everyday life. Holiness is not an ethereal pursuit, or one reserved only for certain citizens in the Church. It is something that God has, by his grace, made attainable for everyone.

PART ONE

Laying the Foundation

CHAPTER 1

Called to Be Saints

Walking through the grounds of a Trappist monastery on a Spring afternoon, I reflected on the profound sense of peace that pervaded the atmosphere. I gazed at the majestic Blue Ridge Mountains towering silently in the distance like massive sentinels protecting the land from modern encroachments. As far as my eye could see, green foliage spread throughout the landscape; the only sounds I heard were the occasional chirping of a bird or lowing of a cow. Having escaped for one weekend from the grind of the "real world," my thoughts ran akin to those of the novice monk Alyosha in *The Brothers Karamazov* when he juxtaposes his monastery with the outside world: "Here was quiet, here was holiness, and there—confusion, and a darkness in which one immediately got lost and went astray."[2] Holiness seemed an attainable dream as I walked among the Trappists—but back in real life? How could holiness go hand in hand with client meetings, diaper changes, and mowing the lawn?

It is precisely in work and family that God has called me to holiness, however, since, of course, I am not a monk. Has God set up an impossible goal for me? Can man reach for holiness while living

[2] Fyodor Dostoevsky, *The Brothers Karamazov*, trans. Richard Pevear and Larissa Volokhonsky (New York: Farrar, Straus, and Giroux, 1990), 157.

in the world? The young Karamazov too faced this dilemma, when the elder monk Zosima commanded him to leave the monastery for the outside world:

> You will go forth from these walls, but you will sojourn in the world like a monk. You will have many opponents, but your very enemies will love you. Life will bring you many misfortunes, but through them you will be happy, and you will bless life and cause others to bless it—which is the most important thing.[3]

For a time Alyosha resisted his elder's command; the monastery seemed to him to be his only path to a holy and peaceful life. But eventually, Alyosha embraced his vocation as a "sojourner" outside the monastery walls:

> Alyosha stood gazing and suddenly, as if he had been cut down, threw himself to the earth. He did not know why he was embracing it, he did not try to understand why he longed so irresistibly to kiss it, to kiss all of it, but he was kissing it, weeping, sobbing, and watering it with his tears, and he vowed ecstatically to love it, to love it unto ages of ages.... He fell to the earth a weak youth and rose up a fighter, steadfast for the rest of his life, and he knew it and felt it suddenly, in that very moment of his ecstasy.... Three days later he left the monastery, which was also in accordance with the words of his late elder, who had bidden him to "sojourn in the world."[4]

The pilgrimage of young Alyosha out of the monastery and into a life of serving God in the world conflicted with his era's common

---

3   Ibid., 285.
4   Ibid., 362–363.

conception of holiness. For in the nineteenth century, the idea that holiness could only be achieved in the religious life pervaded the Christian world—surely a life "in the world" was not meant for growing in sanctity. This view that only in the religious state could one find a path to holiness—although never officially embraced by the Church—was a widely accepted assumption of millions of Catholics. It was for priests or monks or nuns to strive for holiness. A married man or woman should only hope for a minimum of sanctity, just enough to get to Heaven.

But this "two-tiered" concept had not always held sway in the Church. The first centuries of Christianity were marked by a universal ideal of holiness, and many saints and teachers in the Church throughout the centuries continued to emphasize this ideal. Yet the typical Catholic from the time of the early Middle Ages up to the modern era conceived of holiness as something synonymous with the religious life. How is it that this occurred—that the universal call to holiness was lost in the life of the Church?

For lay holiness has deep roots in Christian tradition, beginning with the preaching of Christ, or, to go back even further, with Christianity's Jewish origins. When God gave the Israelites the Law, He commanded, "You shall be holy to me; for I the Lord am holy" (Lev. 20:26). This demand of universal holiness continued in the early Church, as St. Paul wrote to the Ephesians that

> [God] chose us in him before the foundation of the world, that we should be holy and blameless before him. He destined us in love to be his sons through Jesus Christ, according to the purpose of his will, to the praise of his glorious grace which he freely bestowed on us in the Beloved. (Eph. 1:4–6).

From all eternity God desires that each person "be holy and blameless." This is a holiness that is the right and the duty of the children of God, "his sons through Jesus Christ." As St. Paul put it simply to the Thessalonians, "For this is the will of God, your sanctification" (1 Thess. 4:3a).

Furthermore, the holiness we are called to is not reserved for certain occupations or professions, but can be achieved through any noble state of life. Again, St. Paul shows us the way: "Whether you eat or drink, or whatever you do, do all to the glory of God" (1 Cor. 10:31); and, "Whatever you do, in word or deed, do everything in the name of the Lord Jesus" (Col. 3:17). According to the great Apostle to the Gentiles, every action we take can be for God's glory and thus advance us in lives of holiness.

We find the basis for St. Paul's exhortations in the Jewish tradition as well as in the words of Jesus Himself, especially in the Sermon on the Mount (see Matt. 5–7). This "magna carta" of Christian life, it should be noted, was not addressed only to Christ's closest followers, but to "the crowds" (Matt. 5:1). If the Lord had laid out this demanding way of life only to the Apostles, perhaps we would be justified in relegating holiness to a quest of priests and religious. But in directing His words to the crowds, Christ's command is clearly intended for all.

In this Sermon, Christ first insists that certain attitudes are necessary for a holy life: poverty of spirit, gentleness, mercy, and purity (see Matt. 5:1–12). These attitudes will form Christians who, by their lives, are witnesses to the world of a better way of living—they will be salt and light in the world (see Matt. 5:13–16). By focusing on attitudes instead of specific actions at the start of His Sermon, Christ challenges the assumption that external observance of the law is enough; instead, interior reform is necessary (see Matt. 21–47). Holiness is not simply following a set of rules; it is a complete *metanoia*—a total change in life powered by an inner conversion of heart and mind.

Christ's demands are nothing short of extraordinary: "You, there-fore, must be perfect, as your heavenly Father is perfect" (Matt. 5:48). These demands are based, of course, in God's command to "be holy" as He is holy (see Lev. 20:26). God desires perfection for each and every person in each and every walk of life—and although this is humanly impossible to achieve, Christ always pours out His grace to move us closer to perfection.

The universal nature of Christ's demanding call to holiness was not lost on the early Church—anyone who wanted to convert to Christianity knew he was taking his life in his hands. Just going to Mass could be a death sentence. The Roman authorities persecuted all Christians—not just the clergy—so all Christians were con-stantly reminded that their faith was a serious matter. The model of sanctity in these early days of the Church was martyrdom, and Christians from all walks of life—young, old, cleric, or lay—shed their blood for Christ, becoming perfect in their deaths.

But with the conversion of the Roman Empire we start to see the first splintering in the understanding of the universal vocation to holiness. No longer was martyrdom a constant threat to every Christian; now that Christianity was legal—and even the preferred religion—the urgency of the Christian life was lost. Many people were becoming Christian for social and political reasons, adding great numbers to the Church but also creating a wide range of intensity within its ranks.

Of course, there were still many Christians who desired to give their lives totally in some concrete way. Thus the rise of the monas-tics. These men and women physically removed themselves from ordinary life in order to bear witness to the total devotion each person should give to the Lord. While the great teachers of the Church—such as St. Augustine, St. John Chrysostom, and St. Gregory the Great—understood that these monastics were to be models for all Christians and that each person was to give a total commitment in his own state of life, the monastic trend nevertheless marks the birth of the notion that holiness is for the consecrated, not the layman. Those who wished to strive for holiness would consecrate their lives to God in the Church; then there was everyone else, who would simply hope to do enough to make it to Purgatory.

This attitude, which became so deeply entrenched in the Middle Ages, began to weaken in modern times. The first cracks were seen in the rise of the mendicant orders, such as the Franciscans and the Dominicans, during the Middle Ages. The mission of these orders was not to remain in the monastery or convent, but to engage those in the world directly. Although their members were consecrated religious, they did not live in secluded monasteries, but instead preached and taught in the city streets and at universities filled with laymen. Furthermore, these orders spawned "third orders": associations of men and women who followed the spirituality and many of the practices of the order, but remained laypeople in the midst of the world. This infiltration of the religious life into the ordinary world led more and more laypeople to see that holiness was something every person could—and should—strive for.

One of the great examples of a layperson following the call to holiness in the world was St. Thomas More (1478–1535). This English saint, who considered a monastic life before finally discerning a call to marriage and family, did not see the life of a layperson as an obstacle to holiness. Not only did he desire holiness for himself, he was also adamant that all in his household have the same goal. He was rigorous in all aspects of his children's education, but their religious education was always his top priority. All of England knew him to be a man of integrity, and it was due to this reputation that King Henry VIII wanted More's blessing on his illegitimate marriage to Anne Boleyn; for if More supported it, everyone would

CALLED TO BE SAINTS

acknowledge that it must be a holy union. However, More's commitment to complete devotion to the Lord and His Church would not allow him to compromise on this issue, and he was eventually martyred for holding to the truth. Today, his example of lay holiness has made him the patron of politicians and statesmen, as well as an excellent role model for Catholic fathers.

Soon after More went to his eternal reward, St. Francis de Sales (1567–1622) became one of the greatest teachers of lay spirituality to ever grace the Church. His *Introduction to the Devout Life* was specifically directed not to religious, but to laypeople in the midst of the world. He lived in a Catholic culture that continued to separate laypeople from the quest for holiness, but in the preface to this work he writes,

> Almost all who have hitherto treated of devotion have had in view the instruction of persons wholly retired from the world, or at least have taught a kind of devotion leading to this absolute retirement. My intention is to instruct such as live in towns, or families, or at court, and who, by their condition, are obliged to lead, as to externals, the ordinary life. Such persons often will not even consider the question of undertaking the devout life, under pretext of its supposed impossibility in their circumstances, for in their opinion as no beast dares to taste the seed of the herb Palma Christi, so no man ought to aspire to the palm of Christian piety as long as he lives in the bustle of temporal affairs.[5]

De Sales insists that a devout life is possible for everyone: "It is an error, and even a heresy, to endeavour to banish the devout life

---

[5]   St. Francis de Sales, *Introduction to the Devout Life* (New York: Longman, Green, and Co., 1891), 15–16.

from the ranks of soldiers, the shops of tradesmen, the courts of princes, or the households of married people…. Wheresoever we are, we may and ought to aspire to the perfect life."[6]

More recently, people in all walks of life have embraced the spirituality of the Carmelite nun St. Thérèse of Lisieux (1873–1897) — a "little way" to holiness. By recognizing that every action, no matter how small in the eyes of the world, can be an act of love for God, St. Thérèse laid a clear path for holiness in all states of life.

But in spite of the teachings and examples of these great saints, it was still commonplace in the early twentieth century to consider holiness the exclusive domain of those in religious life. It was in this environment that St. Josemaría Escrivá (1902–1975) was born and raised, and it would become his mission to insist that the call to holiness was universal to all peoples and all walks of life. This Spanish saint recognized that many had forgotten the call of our Lord for everyone to be perfect. Early in his ministry St. Josemaría wrote,

> For those who knew how to read the Gospel, how clear was that general call to holiness in ordinary life, in one's profession, without leaving one's own environment! But for many centuries most Christians did not understand this: there was no evidence of the ascetical phenomenon of many people seeking sanctity in this way, staying where they were, sanctifying their work and sanctifying themselves in their work. And soon, by dint of not practicing it, the doctrine was forgotten.[7]

---

6 Ibid., 7.
7 St. Josemaría Escrivá, "Letter, Jan. 9, 1932, no. 95," in *Opus Dei in the Church*, ed. Pedro Rodriguez, Fernando Ocariz, and Jose Luis Illanes (New York: Scepter Publishers, 2003), 114.

The doctrine may have been forgotten, but St. Josemaría witnessed its rediscovery in the Church in the twentieth century. Near the end of his life, the Church officially proclaimed the message he had been insistently preaching. At the Second Vatican Council, held from 1962 to 1965, the council fathers issued a document titled *Lumen Gentium* ("Light of the Nations"), which revolved around the conviction that all members of the Church are called to holiness. Chapter 5 of this document—titled "The Universal Call to Holiness"—declares:

> [All] the faithful of Christ of whatever rank or status, are called to the fullness of the Christian life and to the perfection of charity.... The classes and duties of life are many, but holiness is one—that sanctity which is cultivated by all who are moved by the Spirit of God, and who obey the voice of the Father and worship God the Father in spirit and in truth ... all Christ's faithful, whatever be the conditions, duties, and circumstances of their lives—and indeed through all these, will daily increase in holiness, if they receive all things with faith from the hand of their heavenly Father and if they cooperate with the divine will.[8]

Furthermore, the council stated that holiness could be pursued in all honorable walks of life:

> For all [the laity's] works, prayers, and apostolic endeavors, their ordinary married and family life, their daily occupations, their physical and mental relaxation, if carried out in the Spirit, and even the hardships of life, if

---

[8] Vatican Council II, Dogmatic Constitution on the Church *Lumen gentium* (November 14, 1979), no. 40.

patiently borne—all these become "spiritual sacrifices acceptable to God through Jesus Christ."[9]

The council thus codified what St. Josemaría had been preaching for decades: that every person is called to holiness no matter their vocation or state in life, and that every occupation and profession can be a means to achieve sanctity. St. Josemaría's life work was to call all men and women to recognize their duty to strive for holiness in the world. His passion was to see ordinary people become extraordinary by means of their ordinary work. Joseph Cardinal Ratzinger—the future Pope Benedict XVI—said in a homily for the beatification of St. Josemaría,

> The word "saint" has undergone a dangerous restriction in meaning with the passage of time, which is still very much around. When we think of the saints on the altars, and of miracles and heroic virtues, we regard all that as something reserved for a chosen few among whom we have no place. Let us then leave holiness for these few unknown people and settle for being what we are. Josemaría Escrivá has shaken people out of this spiritual apathy: no, holiness is not an unusual thing; it is something common and normal for all the baptized. It does not involve epic achievements of a vague and unattainable heroism; it assumes countless forms, and can be achieved in any state and condition in life.[10]

The life and teachings of St. Josemaría had one goal: helping every person to become a saint. He insisted, time and time again,

---

9 Ibid., no. 34.
10 Joseph Cardinal Ratzinger, "Homily, May 19, 1992," in *Opus Dei in the Church*, 114.

that we can become saints in our ordinary lives, sanctifying ourselves and the world through work, family life, and all daily activities. Like a real-life Zosima, he knew it was the task of most Christians to "sojourn in the world." My time at the Trappist monastery was wonderful—it's vital to take time out from our usual schedules to reconnect with God. But a quiet monastery is not where God has called me—or most of us—to grow in holiness. It is in the ordinary activities of the everyday—client meetings, changing diapers, and mowing the lawn—that my own personal path to sainthood will be found.

St. Josemaría's life's work was to help all people reach the sanctity to which we are called in whatever vocation, and whatever place, God gives us. Let us next look briefly at the life of this extraordinary man, who saw the ordinary as the means to holiness.

READ

Read chapter 5 — "The Universal Call to Holiness" — of Vatican II's *Lumen Gentium* (available at https://www.vatican.va/archive/hist_councils/ii_vatican_council/documents/vat-ii_const_19641121_lumen-gentium_en.html).

MEDITATE

Meditate on the following from *Lumen Gentium*:

> [A]ll the faithful of Christ of whatever rank or status are called to the fullness of the Christian life and to the perfection of charity. (Lumen Gentium, 40)

- Do I desire the perfection of charity in my life or do I just want to be "good enough"?
- Whom in my life do I fail to see as an image of God?

PRAY

- Ask God for the grace of a holy life.
- Pray that all people might respond to the call to holiness.

CONTEMPLATE

Consider holiness as allowing no longer yourself to live, but Christ to live in you (cf. Galatians 2:20).

Chapter 2

A Modern-Day Saint

Our Lord has raised up in these years his Work because
he wants it never again unknown or forgotten that all
are called to strive for sanctity, and that the majority of
Christians are called to do this in the world, in ordinary work. For that reason, as long as there are people
on this earth, the Work will exist. There will always be
persons of every profession and position who seek
sanctity within their state of life, within that profession
or position of theirs; contemplative souls in the midst
of the world.[11]

Thus did St. Josemaría Escrivá describe his mission in life, confidently
trusting in the Lord to accomplish this "Opus Dei," or "Work of
God." But how did this Spanish priest come to know so clearly what
it was that God wanted from him? How did God call this man—someone who was born in comfort, but was then quickly thrust into
suffering and poverty; who begged the Lord for years to reveal His
plan to him with no answer—how did God reveal to him His

---

[11] Josemaría Escrivá, "Letter, Jan. 9, 1932, no. 92," in *The Founder
of Opus Dei: The Life of Josemaría Escrivá, Volume I*, ed. Andrés
Vázquez de Prada (New York: Scepter Publishers, 2001), 261.

mission to remind the Church that all people are equally called to sanctity, no matter their state in life or profession?

Josemaría Escrivá de Balaguer was born to an upper-middle-class, devoutly Catholic family on January 9, 1902, in Barbastro, Spain. His father was a successful businessman, and young Josemaría was the second child of the family, following a sister.

When Josemaría was about two years old, he became seriously ill, and his parents and the family doctor all believed he was going to die. One night his illness became so severe that death appeared imminent. His doctor, in fact, came the next morning and asked, "What time did the boy die?" Unbeknownst to him, Josemaría's parents had begun a novena to Our Lady and promised a pilgrimage to her shrine in nearby Torreciudad if he was cured; the boy completely recovered. In later years, Josemaría's mother would often recall to Josemaría that he had been "more dead than alive" and conclude that the Blessed Mother must have something great in mind for him.

For a number of years following this near-death episode, the Escrivá family lived a comfortable and happy life, welcoming three new daughters in quick succession. However, this pleasant family situation ended abruptly when Josemaría was only eight years old. His youngest sister died before her first birthday. Over the next three years, his two other younger sisters also died. These tragic deaths had a profound effect on the young Josemaría, who, after the third death of a sister, remarked to his mother, "Next year it's my turn." In addition to these tragedies, his father faced serious problems with his business, leading to bankruptcy. So in the span of less than five years, the Escrivá family went from a comfortable living situation to emotional turmoil and financial collapse.

The response of Josemaría's parents to these events, however, would have a deep impact on the young boy: they neither complained nor blamed God for their calamities. Josemaría's father did everything he could to repay all his creditors (although he had not been the cause of the failure of the business), and he took any job he could to support his family. This naturally entailed the Escrivá family moving to a more modest dwelling and embarking on a significantly reduced standard of living.

All through this time, the family continued to live a devout Catholic life. Josemaría received his First Communion and practiced the normal acts of piety for a Spanish Catholic of the time. He appeared destined to become a professional and a family man. However, one day shortly before his sixteenth birthday, he had an experience that would change the course of his life. In his town there were stationed two Discalced Carmelite priests who lived an austere life of prayer, fasting, and, as their name suggests, going about with bare feet. One winter day, Josemaría saw in the snow footprints that had been made by one of the shoeless Carmelites. Moved by this scene, he asked himself, "If others can make such sacrifices for God and neighbor, can't I offer him something?" Shortly thereafter, he made the decision to become a priest.

However, because as a priest in a religious order he would have been unable to support his family, Josemaría, being the oldest son and feeling obligated to this responsibility, did not become a member of the Carmelites or any other religious community; instead he entered the diocesan seminary to become a priest for the city of Saragossa, for diocesan priests were better able to care for their families. But Josemaría was still concerned. As the only son, he would be financially responsible for his parents as they aged: Might not being a priest, as opposed to a lawyer or doctor, keep him from doing this? With the gumption peculiar to the ardently faithful, Josemaría's solution was to pray that his parents would have another son. Such a "solution" was backed only by faith, for not only was his mother over forty years old, she had not had a child in ten years. After making this prayer, however, Josemaría considered the matter settled.

Less than a year later, his mother gave birth to a son. Although Josemaría was sure of his call to the priesthood, in the early years of his seminary life and immediately following his ordination, he also felt that God was calling him to something more. He knew that God wanted him—and his priesthood—for some specific task, but was ignorant of what it might be. So, for almost ten years, he cried out over and over the prayer of the blind man, *"Domine, ut videam!"* (Lord, that I may see!). The young priest begged the Lord to reveal to him the plan He had for his life. He knew the life of a simple diocesan priest was a noble one, but he also knew with certainty that God wanted something more from him.

Finally, on October 2, 1928, the Lord answered his prayer. That autumn day, which saw the celebration of the feast of the Guardian Angels, Fr. Josemaría was on retreat and had returned to his room to write some notes and recollect his thoughts. Suddenly, he had a vision in which he "saw" his mission: a movement in which millions of people would sanctify their lives through ordinary work, while living in the midst of the world. He never fully explained what he saw, but he always considered October 2, 1928, as the day of the founding of what would later be called *Opus Dei*, the "Work of God." This was the beginning of what became his life's work.

This October vision was the first in a series of mystical experiences Fr. Josemaría would have in the next few years that would shape his entire life and influence the lives of millions of people around the world. Of note, however, is that he refused to flaunt these experiences or exploit them for his advantage. In fact, he often downplayed them, keeping the focus completely on his mission. Fr. Josemaría knew that such experiences are frequently misunderstood—bringing more attention to the recipient of the visions than to their message. Nevertheless, these visions would mold his understanding of his work until his death more than fifty years later.

The next vision occurred on February 14, 1930. Up to this point, Fr. Josemaría assumed that his movement would consist only of men—he did not feel that God was calling him to lead women in this work of God. But while celebrating Mass in a small chapel in Madrid, he had a mystical vision of the women's branch of Opus Dei. He realized that since both men and women were called to holiness in the midst of the world, his work would benefit both. He immediately took this vision to his confessor, and it was confirmed that his message of sanctifying ordinary life should be extended to women. The acceptance of women in the movement became a confirmation to Fr. Josemaría that this work was truly God's and not his own. As he later wrote, "I said, 'I don't want women in Opus Dei!' and God said, 'Well, I do.'"[12]

The vision of women in his movement was not the last insight Fr. Josemaría would receive from God regarding his work. A little over a year later, on August 7, 1931, Fr. Josemaría was celebrating Mass for the Feast of the Transfiguration. At the elevation of the Host, he heard a voice, which declared: *"Et ego, si exaltatus fuero a terra, omnia traham ad me ipsum!"* ["And I, when I am lifted up from the earth, will draw all things to myself"] (John 12:32). In the context of St. John's Gospel, this passage reflects Christ's desire that his being "lifted up" on the Cross will bring about the redemption of all mankind. But Fr. Josemaría was struck by another meaning of the passage, one that would guide him throughout his life:

> The time for the Consecration arrived. At the very moment when I elevated the Sacred Host ... there came to my mind, with extraordinary force and clarity, that passage of

---

[12] Josemaría Escrivá, "Personal Notes, no. 1871," in *The Founder of Opus Dei: The Life of Josemaría Escrivá, Volume I*, ed. Andrés Vázquez de Prada (New York: Scepter Publishers, 2001), 278.

Scripture, *Et ego, si exaltatus fuero a terra, omnia traham ad me ipsum*. And I understood that there will be men and women of God who will lift the cross, with the teachings of Christ, to the pinnacle of all human activities.... And I saw our Lord triumph, attracting to him all things.[13]

Fr. Josemaría recognized in this insight the driving force behind his preaching: all human activities would be lifted up to the Cross, united with it, and be the means by which the salvation of souls would be accomplished. There would be no distinction between "sacred" activities and "secular" ones—all the activities of man could be united to Christ's triumph.

One more otherworldly experience would occur shortly thereafter that would crystallize for Fr. Josemaría another reality that guided his whole ministry: the recognition that we are all sons and daughters of God. He wrote in his journal:

Feast of Saint Hedwig [October 16], 1931: I wanted to pray, after Mass, in the quiet of my church. I didn't succeed. On Atocha Street I bought a newspaper and got on the streetcar. Up to this moment, when I'm writing this, I have not been able to read more than one paragraph of the paper. I have felt flowing through me a prayer of copious and ardent feelings of affection. That's the way it was in the streetcar and all the way home. What I am doing now, this note, is really a continuation. I only interrupt this prayer to exchange a few words with my family... and to kiss my Blessed Virgin of the Kisses, and our Child Jesus.[14]

[13]   Ibid., 326–327.
[14]   Josemaría Escrivá, "Personal Notes, no. 334," in *The Founder of Opus Dei: The Life of Josemaría Escrivá, Volume I*, ed. Andrés Vázquez de Prada (New York: Scepter Publishers, 2001), 333.

What were the details of that prayer of "copious and ardent feelings of affection?" Fr. Josemaría would later explain,

> I felt the action of the Lord. He was making spring forth in my heart and on my lips, with the force of something imperatively necessary, this tender invocation: Abba! Pater! I was out on the street, in a streetcar.... Probably I made that prayer out loud. And I walked the streets of Madrid for maybe an hour, maybe two, I can't say; time passed without my being aware of it. They must have thought I was crazy. I was contemplating, with lights that were not mine, that amazing truth. It was like a lighted coal burning in my soul, never to be extinguished.[15]

Fr. Josemaría would again and again return to this truth: the earth-shattering—yet too often taken for granted—fact that we are children of God, and that the Creator of the universe is our loving Father. To Fr. Josemaría, this reality was not simply a pleasant thought or a comforting notion: it was to form the foundation for all his efforts to teach laypeople how to become holy in the midst of the world.

Over the next decade, Fr. Josemaría worked tirelessly to make what he saw in these visions a reality, but without much success. Although several people expressed initial enthusiasm for what Fr. Josemaría was doing, most eventually fell away. At the time, the idea of being "religious" meant, well, being a religious. But Fr. Josemaría's idea was radically different: it entailed striving for sanctity as much as any priest or religious, but doing it in the world. In fact, Fr. Josemaría met with much resistance from many priests and religious, because they felt that he was working against them

---

[15] Escrivá, "Personal Notes, no. 60," in *The Founder of Opus Dei,* 334.

and pulling vocations from them—if you tell people they can be holy out in the world, who will enter our seminaries and convents? Fr. Josemaría accepted with resignation this misguided opposition and insisted that his followers never attack or demean any priests or other ecclesial figures who might be opposed to their work. Fr. Josemaría, of course, greatly respected the religious life and the priesthood, but he knew that the majority of people needed a way to become holy in the midst of the secular world, not apart from it. As he once wrote in his personal notes, "Ordinary Christians. A fermenting mass. Ours is the ordinary, with naturalness. Medium: professional work. All saints!"[16]

Fr. Josemaría's struggles in recruiting for Opus Dei became even more difficult with the advent of the Spanish Civil War. The few existing members of the fledgling group were scattered throughout the country, and Fr. Josemaría himself was caught in the Republican Zone where priests were hunted down and often martyred. He avoided capture by hiding in various places, including a mental institution and the Honduran Embassy.

During this time, many of Fr. Josemaría's friends and his family urged him to try to escape to the safety of the Nationalist Zone. But the priest resisted, for he did not want to leave his loved ones in danger while he fled from it. He prayed and prayed for guidance and finally decided to attempt escape. But even as he was working his way to the Nationalist Zone, he still doubted whether he was following God's will by fleeing.

At one point in his journey, his group stopped in an abandoned barn filled with rats and mice. The other men slept soundly, for their

16 Josemaría Escrivá, "Personal Notes, no. 35," in *Holiness and the World: Studies in the Teaching of Blessed Josemaria Escriva*, ed. M. Belda, J. Escudero, J. L. Illanes, and P. O'Callaghan (Scepter Publishing,1997), 211.

journey had been exhausting, but Fr. Josemaría could not sleep, for he was filled with concern for those he had left behind. He became convinced that he was not being faithful to God's will and resolved to return back home. But the others in his group insisted that he continue, despite his protests. So they moved on to the abandoned rectory of a small parish church, where Fr. Josemaría continued to pray and beg the Lord for guidance. At one point the other men heard the priest sobbing, convinced that he should return. Eventually he ceased to cry, but continued to pray. He beseeched Mary's intercession to calm his conscience and make clear for him the way he should follow. After a time, he went downstairs to the sacristy, but shortly returned, filled with joy and completely refreshed. What had happened to cause this sudden reversal? He had found a gilded wooden rose, and he immediately took it as a sign from our Lady that he was doing the right thing. He announced that he would celebrate Mass, and then he continued on his journey to safety and freedom. Eventually, Fr. Josemaría and his group were able to escape to the Nationalist Zone via a perilous trek through the Pyrenees Mountains. As soon as he reached safety, Fr. Josemaría began to work again to build up Opus Dei, which had by then become almost nonexistent. Most of his original members were in one of the two competing armies, or were inaccessible to him in the Republican Zone. Undaunted, Fr. Josemaría journeyed tirelessly throughout the Nationalist Zone during the rest of the Civil War, visiting countless people and encouraging all to sanctify their lives, even in the midst of the pain and suffering of war.

It was shortly after the war's end that the book Fr. Josemaría is most known for was published. Earlier in the decade a small book of his reflections called *Consideraciones espirituales* had a limited publication. It consisted of spiritual points for consideration that Fr. Josemaría had written over the years in letters to friends, in personal journals, and in other notes of spiritual advice. In 1939, Fr.

Josemaría decided to take many of these points, plus many others he had written in the interval, and publish nine hundred-ninety-nine of them in one book, which was entitled *Camino* ("The Way").

Encapsulating Fr. Josemaría's path to becoming a saint in ordinary life, the spiritual points contained in *The Way* are at once practical and demanding. For example, "Say to your body: 'I would rather keep you in slavery than be myself your slave.' "[17] Little nuggets of spiritual advice like this were easily accessible to the average person. The book quickly rose in popularity, serving to spread Fr. Josemaría's message throughout Spain. Eventually, *The Way* became one of the most popular spiritual books of the twentieth century, being translated into more than forty languages and selling more than four million copies worldwide.

After the end of the Civil War, Opus Dei began to grow by leaps and bounds. Quickly it expanded into other countries, and soon Fr. Josemaría decided to seek permission to have a few members of Opus Dei ordained as priests so that its members would be able to receive spiritual guidance from priests who had thoroughly embraced their spirituality.

Fr. Josemaría envisioned Opus Dei as a universal phenomenon in the Church and, recognizing Rome as the heart of the Church, wanted to make the Eternal City the headquarters of his movement. So in 1946 he moved to Rome. As we will see, it was very important to Fr. Josemaría to be thoroughly "Roman." After his move, Opus Dei continued to expand throughout the world. As the work of Fr. Josemaría spread, his message of holiness in everyday life became more widely accepted in the Church. More and more, Catholics

---

[17] Josemaria Escriva, *The Way*, no. 214 (New York: Image Reprint, 2007), 35. Available at https://www.escrivaworks.org/book/the_way.htm

began to recognize that holiness was not just for priests and religious, but for everyone. Fr. Josemaría's core message received official Church support when Vatican II enshrined that belief in *Lumen Gentium* chapter 5, a chapter entitled "The Universal Call to Holiness."

Josemaría Escrivá died in Rome on June 26, 1975. Shortly after his death, the cause for his sainthood was opened, and just seventeen years after he passed to the next world the Church beatified him. Ten years later, on October 6, 2002, Pope John Paul II, in front of thousands of people crammed into St. Peter's Square, declared him to be St. Josemaría Escrivá, a "saint of ordinary life."

Read

Read the chapter "Why Opus Dei?" in *Conversation with St. Josemaría Escrivá* (available free online at https://www.escrivaworks.org).

Meditate

Meditate on this quote from St. Josemaría Escrivá:

"If others can make such sacrifices for God and neighbor, can't I offer him something?"

- What does it mean to be a saint in the modern world?
- What can I offer to God in my life?

Pray

- Pray for those who strive for holiness in the midst of the world today.
- Ask God to make clear what He wants from you in this life.

Contemplate

What does it mean to be a saint in the modern world?

Chapter 3

Abba! Father!

Imagine overhearing the following conversation in a Catholic rectory:

"Father Woods, do you want me to print out this letter from the Holy Father about the Blessed Mother?"

"Yes, Sister Bernadette, I want to insert it in this week's bulletin. By the way, let's contact Mother Lucia about having another sister come for the parish mission."

This short slice of Catholic life is seeped in familial titles—Father, Mother, Sister. And here we have a fundamental characteristic of the Catholic Faith: the Church is a family. By virtue of our baptism, we are children of God—all brothers and sisters with one common Father. We call Mary the "Blessed Mother," our priests are "fathers" to us, the members of the religious are "brothers," "sisters," and "mothers," and we even call the Pope our "Holy Father." The idea that we are all one big family of God is integral to the Catholic understanding of our Christian Faith. Yet often we take this reality for granted: we lose sight of the fact that the all-powerful, all-holy Creator God is our Father, and we neglect to think of ourselves as children of this Father.

We are children of God. This tenet, called divine filiation, formed the basis of St. Josemaría's teachings on becoming holy in the world. It is not an exaggeration to say that the concept of divine filiation forms the very foundation of his entire spirituality—and is the key that unlocks the door to growth in holiness. It is because God is our Father that we receive His very life of holiness; it is because we are children of a loving Father that we should submit ourselves to His will in humility; it is because we are sons of God and brothers with Christ that we should model our very lives on the eternal Son of God, Jesus Christ. These three threads—God's divine paternity, our spiritual childhood, and our sonship with Christ—intertwine to form St. Josemaría's profound teaching on divine filiation and lay out the path to holiness in the world.

Our Father God

Perhaps no parable has captured the imagination of generations of Christians more than that of the Prodigal Son. This story has touched hearts in diverse cultures throughout the centuries because it illustrates the unbounded love of God. In fact, it could be named instead the "Parable of the Merciful Father," for it is the father who drives the action and touches our hearts. He pours forth on his son a reckless love—he first gives him his inheritance before the proper time, and then after it is squandered, enthusiastically welcomes his son back into the family fold. And when the older brother complains of his father's generosity, the father only mildly scolds him, reminding the older boy that "everything I own is yours" (Luke 15:11–32). Every action of the father in this story reaches outward; there is no selfishness or smallness in his love for his sons—everything that he is and has he lavishly gives to them, for they are in all things his heirs. The moral of the story is that God our Father pours all that is His upon His children unreservedly.

This realization came to St. Josemaría powerfully in a supernatural way in one word: "Abba." This Aramaic word, which was used by Jesus when referring to God as His father, was impressed upon the Spanish saint and stayed with him his whole life:

> I felt the action of the Lord. He was making spring forth in my heart and on my lips, with the force of something imperatively necessary, this tender invocation: Abba! Pater! I was out on the street, in a streetcar.... Probably I made that prayer out loud. And I walked the streets of Madrid for maybe an hour, maybe two. I can't say; time passed without my being aware of it. They must have thought I was crazy. I was contemplating, with lights that were not mine, that amazing truth. It was like a lighted coal burning in my soul, never to be extinguished.[18]

God is our Abba! What a wonderful condescension on the part of God! This realization remained alive in St. Josemaría's heart like a "lighted coal," but most of us would have to admit that our awe regarding this truth is less than it should be.

If we look at the history of human spirituality, we see three primary views of God's relation to mankind. The first sees Him as the supreme Creator who looks on us as an artist looks at his painting or an architect views a building of his design. The second notion sees God as a Master: He looks down upon us as servants or slaves here to do His bidding. But the third way is the Christian's view—that God sees us as His beloved children. Although the difference between God and His creatures is absolute—we are as nothing compared to Him—He has indeed made us His children; we are not His slaves, servants, or possessions. These three views lead to radically different ways of responding to God: the slave or servant will never respond in the same way as a son.

---

[18] Josemaría Escrivá, "Personal Notes, no. 60, December 8, 1949," in *The Founder of Opus Dei*, 334.

A child of God treats the Lord as his Father. He is not obsequious and servile, he is not merely formal and well-mannered: he is completely sincere and trusting. Men do not scandalise God. He can put up with all our infidelities. Our Father in heaven pardons any offence when his child returns to him, when he repents and asks for pardon. The Lord is such a good Father that he anticipates our desire to be pardoned and comes forward to us, opening his arms laden with grace.[19]

Every time we sin, we separate ourselves from our loving Father simply by our action. But often we go beyond that—imagining that God must be disappointed in us, perhaps even angry with us, we turn even further away from Him in shame and guilt. But what loving father would reject his children for the mistakes they have made? Likewise, when we fall, our heavenly Father runs to us in compassion, desiring more than anything to make us whole again.

This reality of divine filiation led St. Paul to proclaim,

> For all who are led by the Spirit of God are sons of God. For you did not receive the spirit of slavery to fall back into fear, but you have received the spirit of sonship. When we cry, "Abba! Father!" it is the Spirit himself bearing witness with our spirit that we are children of God, and if children, then heirs, heirs of God and fellow heirs with Christ, provided we suffer with him in order that we may also be glorified with him. (Rom. 8:14–17)

Inheritance was an important aspect of family life in the ancient world—much more so than today. When the head of a household

---

[19] Escrivá, *Christ is Passing By* (New York: Scepter Publishing, 2017), 64.

passed away, everything he owned went to his firstborn son. St. Paul is telling us that we are all God's "firstborn sons," so we all inherit everything that is God's. What does this divine inheritance include? St. Josemaría exclaims,

> Divine Filiation: I am a son of God!—Consequences: everything belonging to my Father is mine: *ad majora natus sum*: his Mother, his sacraments, his Church, his angels, his Heaven.[20]

Everything that belongs to God—which is truly everything in creation, now belongs to us. But the lavishness of God's bequest to his children goes even further. St. John writes,

> See what love the Father has given us, that we should be called children of God; and so we are. The reason why the world does not know us is that it did not know him. Beloved, we are God's children now; it does not yet appear what we shall be, but we know that when he appears we shall be like him, for we shall see him as he is. (1 John 3:1–2)

We will be like Him: what an amazing gift! God even gives His children His very divine life so that we can become "partakers of the divine nature" (2 Pet. 1:4) and become, as the Eastern Fathers said, "divinized."

> We must live by faith. We must grow in faith—up to the point when it will be possible to describe any one of us, or any Christian, in the terms used by one of the great

---

[20] Escrivá, "Retreat Talk, Jan. 25, 1938," in *The Way: A Critical-Historical Edition*, ed. Pedro Rodríguez (New York: Scepter Publishers, 2009), 452.

Doctors of the eastern Church: "In the same way as transparent bodies, upon receiving a ray of light, become resplendent and shine out, so the souls that are borne and illuminated by the Holy Spirit become themselves spiritual and carry to others the light of grace. From the Holy Spirit comes knowledge of future events, understanding of mysteries, comprehension of hidden truths, giving of gifts, heavenly citizenship, conversation with the angels. From him comes never-ending joy, perseverance in God, likeness to God, and the most sublime state that can be conceived, becoming God-like."

Together with humility, the realization of the greatness of man's dignity—and of the overwhelming fact that, by grace, we are made children of God—forms a single attitude. It is not our own forces that save us and give us life; it is the grace of God. This is a truth which can never be forgotten. If it were, the divinization of our life would be perverted and would become presumption, pride. And this would lead, sooner or later, to a breakdown of spiritual life, when the soul came face to face with its own weakness and wretchedness.[21]

Genesis tells us that when God created all the things of this world, He saw that they were "good" (Gen. 1:1–25). But when He created man, God said, "Let us make man in our image, after our likeness" (Gen. 1:26). In other words, the human race is not merely "good," but like God, who is all-holy. However, because of Original Sin and the Fall, this likeness to God became deformed and stained. But God, in His endless mercy, sent His Son to become man so

---

[21] Escrivá, *Christ is Passing By,* 133.

that our original purpose—to be God's true image and likeness—might be restored. What the Fall deformed, Christ reforms!
St. Athanasius wrote, "the Son of God became man so that men
might become sons of God." What an incredible inheritance: complete transformation into true sons and daughters of God!

Holiness—which leads to divinization—begins with this realization: God is our Father. Holiness is not a matter of following
certain rules set down by a superior. Nor is it a predestined result
that God determines for certain members of His creation. Holiness,
rather, is a living relationship between a loving child who wants
to please his father and a father who gives his child everything he
needs to succeed.

Heirs to a King

The fact that God is our Father means that we are His children.
In other words, we should recognize not only God's fatherly love
for us, but also our place as children of the Father. A son or daughter
of a king is uniquely privileged—but bears a demanding load of
responsibility as a result of his or her lineage. Just so, as children
of God we are called to act in accord with our nobility. Humble
submission to the will of our Father will mark us as true children.
Jesus made spiritual childhood a requirement for His followers:
"Truly, I say to you, unless you turn and become like children, you
will never enter the kingdom of heaven" (Matt. 18:3). One of St.
Josemaría's near-contemporaries, St. Thérèse of Lisieux, placed
spiritual childhood at the center of her spirituality. St. Josemaría
was devoted to St. Thérèse's "little way," encouraging others to see
in the Little Flower the perfect example of someone who became
"small" in order to become great in the ways of God.

The two key aspects of spiritual childhood are abandonment
and submission. "The way of childhood. Abandonment. Spiritual

childhood. All this is not utter nonsense, but a sturdy and solid Christian life."[22] Christians must be like little children, who trust completely that their parents will care for them and protect them. A whole host of anxieties might dominate the mind of an adult: How will I pay my mortgage? How will I care for my aging parents? How can I keep my children safe from the dangers of this world?

When my children were young, I struggled with the knowledge that, unlike my own parents, I would not be able to pay for my children's future college education. I had been raised with the assumption that this was a parent's responsibility, but realized that I was going to fall short of it. I shared this with a priest during spiritual direction, and he bluntly told me that I would have to "get over it" and recognize that in the world we live in, it was almost impossible for a middle-class sole wage-earner with more than a couple children to pay for college. But he reminded me that God is a loving Father who cares for my children more than I ever could. The good Lord will ensure that my children will be educated as is best for their individual vocations. I should not be anxious, he told me, about things I cannot control, but rely on God's providence as a little child relies on his father's.

A little child does not concern himself with worldly anxieties: he trusts unreservedly that his parents will solve any problems he may encounter. "Being a child, you'll have no cares; children quickly forget what troubles them and return to their usual games. With abandonment, therefore, you won't have to worry, for you will rest in the Father."[23] Life entails certain responsibilities, and one cannot abandon them in some flight of spiritual fancy. But there is a crucial difference between responsibilities and anxieties. After the Our

[22] Escrivá, *The Way*, 853.
[23] Ibid., 864.

Father during the Mass, the priest adds the prayer, "Deliver us, Lord, from every evil, and grant us peace in our day. In your mercy keep us free from sin and *protect us from all anxiety* as we wait in joyful hope for the coming of our Savior, Jesus Christ" (emphasis added). Even a little child might have certain responsibilities—cleaning his room or washing the dishes. But he does not have anxieties, because in his simplicity he knows that his parents will take care of everything for him. Likewise, we must not allow our responsibilities to become anxieties, but instead trust that our heavenly Father always cares for our needs.

This trust is most often put to the test when it comes to financial matters. Our culture blurs the distinction between needs and wants. We are told that we need a large yard or a new TV. If we do not have these things, our lives are not complete. Then, when we cannot afford such luxuries, we become anxious and lose our peace. And sometimes we get anxious over financial burdens that are selfless in nature: a college education for our children or care for our elderly parents. No matter the source, however, surely God will care for our needs, will He not?

> Therefore I tell you, do not be anxious about your life, what you shall eat or what you shall drink, nor about your body, what you shall put on. Is not life more than food, and the body more than clothing? Look at the birds of the air: they neither sow nor reap nor gather into barns, and yet your heavenly Father feeds them. Are you not of more value than they? And which of you by being anxious can add one cubit to his span of life? And why are you anxious about clothing? Consider the lilies of the field, how they grow; they neither toil nor spin; yet I tell you, even Solomon in all his glory was not arrayed like one of these. But if God so clothes the grass

of the field, which today is alive and tomorrow is thrown into the oven, will he not much more clothe you, O men of little faith? Therefore do not be anxious, saying, 'What shall we eat?' or 'What shall we drink?' or 'What shall we wear?' For the Gentiles seek all these things; and your heavenly Father knows that you need them all. But seek first his kingdom and his righteousness, and all these things shall be yours as well. (Matt. 6:25–33)

Of all of Christ's commands, perhaps none is more difficult to follow than that simple "do not be anxious about your life." When the pressures of life bombard us, how can we not be anxious? Spiritual childhood is the answer—trust in our loving Father to care for us no matter our situation in life.

Although it is often written (even in this book) that each person should "strive" for holiness, it would be more appropriate to say that we should "abandon" ourselves to holiness. Holiness is not something we attain, but something given to us. This should not lead us to believe, however, that we have no part in our quest for holiness. In order to be holy, we do need to cooperate with the graces given to us by God. Like little children, we must trust our heavenly Father to give us all we need to become like Him. After all, did not Jesus say, "What father among you, if his son asks for a fish, will instead of a fish give him a serpent; or if he asks for an egg, will give him a scorpion? If you then, who are evil, know how to give good gifts to your children, how much more will the heavenly Father give the Holy Spirit to those who ask him!" (Luke 11:11–13). If we desire holiness, we can receive it from God our Father, for He desires it for us even more. By abandoning ourselves to His will each moment as a child abandons himself to his father or mother, we can be confident that God will make us holy by His own means.

Being childlike is not easy, however. Our fallen natures resist submitting themselves, and they desire nothing more than to be in control; we all want to be independent adults. But a child submits to those in authority. This is no less true for spiritual children:

> Spiritual childhood demands submission of the mind, more difficult than submission of the will. In order to subject our mind we need not only God's grace, but also the continual exercise of our will, which says "no" again and again, just as it says "no" to the flesh.[24]

St. Thérèse stressed the idea of becoming "small" in order to humbly follow the will of God; St. Josemaría, too, sees the importance of this submitting attitude, in both mind and will. Note well, however, that by "submission" neither St. Thérèse nor St. Josemaría means the submission of a slave to a master, such as can be found in Islam (a word that means "submission"). Quite the contrary: Christian submission is always linked to spiritual childhood; it is the loving submission of a child who knows his father loves him and who trusts him completely, not the servile submission of someone who fears punishment from his master.

Nor is this the submission of the weak: "Whoever wants to follow this 'little' way in order to become a child, needs to add strength and virility to his will."[25] To the modern mind, this seems like a paradox, for we exalt those who are independent and in control, and reject those who depend upon others. However, it takes "strength and virility" to submit the mind and the will to God our Father. The easy path in life is the one that simply follows our disordered passions and desires. Real strength lies in choosing God's way—which is

---

[24] Escrivá, *The Way*, 856.
[25] Ibid., 856.

often difficult and hard to understand—assured that it is the way that leads to true contentment and fulfillment.

This kind of submission can be especially difficult in the vocation of marriage. In writing about individual roles in marriage, St. Paul first established this underlying principle: "Be subject to one another out of reverence for Christ" (Eph. 5:21). Husbands and wives have their distinct roles in marriage, but at all times they are to be subject to one another. Our fallen natures, however, rebel against any submission, even—and sometimes especially—to our spouses. The "little things" of daily life can be particularly challenging to spouses' submission to one another—things as seemingly minor as who does what chores or when to turn off the nightstand light. But these apparently inconsequential negotiations make up the stuff of a holy life. Do we allow our spouses to get their way in such matters, or do we always have to come out ahead? We're kidding ourselves if we think we can submit to God while refusing to submit to other people. The one who wants to submit to God in big things needs to first learn to submit to Him in these little things, and the primary way we submit to God in everyday life is by submitting to the fallen people He has placed in our lives.

This willingness to submit to others may be exemplified strikingly in long-married couples. My own parents were married for more than sixty-five years, and their commitment—and submission—to one another was a great blessing in my life, and a beautiful witness for my children. What Hollywood might call boring and deadening—Mom making meals lovingly every day for my dad, or Dad faithfully taking care of the bills over the years—was actually a case of being fully as God intends man to be: submissive to our vocations and to each other. Marriages like my parents' are the stuff that holiness is made of.

Sons in the Son

How can we become true sons of God? Look to the eternal Son of God, Jesus Christ. St. Thomas Aquinas said that we are to be "sons in the Son"—we are to model our sonship after the sonship of Christ. As the Second Person of the Blessed Trinity, Christ is the Son of God by His very nature, and it is by grace that we, too, become children of God, with Christ as our perfect model. St. Josemaría liked to say that each Christian is an *alter Christus, ipse Christus*—"another Christ, Christ Himself." Every Christian is called to conform his life to Christ's, and even—as St. Paul wrote—be able to say that it is "no longer I who live, but Christ who lives in me" (Gal. 2:20).

Again, being holy is not simply a matter of being "good"; it is a matter of being like Christ. "To be holy isn't easy, but it isn't difficult either. To be holy is to be a good Christian, to resemble Christ. The more closely a person resembles Christ, the more Christian he is, the more he belongs to Christ, the holier he is."[26] Identification with Christ is the cornerstone of divine filiation. Each Christian is to be what the name implies: a "little Christ." But what does it mean to identify with Christ? How does one do that?

The Christian becomes another Christ when he joins his life to the saving work of Jesus. And when we recall that every action of Christ's was redemptive, it opens the door for us to see that our every moment, every breath, can be offered lovingly to our Lord with the prayer that He grafts it—us—onto His eternal sacrifice. Most Christians focus only on the Passion and death of Christ when they think of redemption, but St. Josemaría correctly emphasized that every action of the God-man was part of the plan of

---

[26] Josemaría Escrivá, *The Forge,* (New York: Scepter Publishing, 2002), 10.

redemption—even those that were hidden from others. Christ gave His whole life for our salvation, and that life included His conception, birth, childhood—everything that encompassed His life was made an offering to the Father on the Cross.

By identifying with Christ, we become part of this work of redemption. Every action in our lives, if united to Christ, can be offered to our Father for the redemption of the world. Christ offered up His human sonship—His submission and obedience to a mother and father He created—for our salvation. He offered each job he had as a carpenter for the salvation of souls. We, too, must offer up our relationships and work to God in union with His Son.

This is the mystery of the Incarnation. Although Christ always knew where His life was leading, that did not make His sacrifice any less difficult. And His was a total sacrifice—of family, of friends, and of a peaceful life. He grew up in a loving family with a devoted mother, and He had many close and caring friends. By accepting the mission His Father gave him, He gave up any possibility of human happiness and peace. And as a true man, He was surely attracted to such happiness. Yet He knew that any happiness outside of God's will was superficial, so He willingly gave it up, all in obedience to His heavenly Father and out of love for His fellow man.

Ultimately, Christ's greatest offering was on Calvary: the offering of His life on the Cross. The offering of our lives, therefore, will also involve suffering. Some might object that a loving father would attempt to hold back, if he could, the experience of suffering from his children, but this is not the way of God our Father. He allows suffering so that we might grow in holiness and grace. His Son Jesus underwent suffering in order to be our salvation: "For it was fitting that he, for whom and by whom all things exist, in bringing many sons to glory, should make the pioneer of their salvation perfect through suffering" (Heb. 2:10). St. Paul ties suffering directly to sonship when he writes, "When we cry, 'Abba! Father!' it is the Spirit Himself bearing witness with our spirit that we are children of God, and if children, then heirs, heirs of God and fellow heirs with Christ, provided we suffer with him in order that we may also be glorified with him" (Rom. 8:15–17).

St. Paul wrote, "I rejoice in my sufferings for your sake, and in my flesh I complete what is lacking in Christ's afflictions for the sake of his body, that is, the church" (Col. 1:24). Paul became so united to Christ that his sufferings became part of the sufferings offered by Christ in the eternal sacrifice of the Cross. All the children of God, led by the eternal Son of God, unite their lives in one fragrant offering to God our Father. The only way to share in the glory of the Son of God—to receive our inheritance—is to share also in His sufferings.

> God is my Father, even though he may send me suffering. He loves me tenderly, even while wounding me. Jesus suffers, to fulfil the Will of the Father.... And I, who also wish to fulfil the most holy Will of God, following in the footsteps of the Master, can I complain if I too meet suffering as my travelling companion? It will be a sure sign of my sonship, because God is treating me as he treated his own Divine Son.[27]

When suffering comes, it is not because God has abandoned us, it is because He is treating us as sons. By imitating Christ, we can take these moments of suffering—which can span years in some cases—and offer them to the Father, thus participating in the redemption wrought by Christ.

---

[27] Josemaría Escrivá, "*The Way of the Cross,* First Station," Josemaria Escriva Works, accessed June 28, 2022, https://www.escrivaworks. org/book/the_way_of_the_cross-point-1.htm.

In order to make this offering, however, we must have an accurate conception of what suffering is. We read the stories of the saints and their incredible sacrifices, and we are inspired to emulate them exactly. We might dream of going to a foreign land and serving the poor and needy. But suffering is usually less sensational, made up of the multitude of setbacks and tragedies that affect human life. Our first response to this kind of suffering is usually resistance. We might resent being passed over for a promotion in favor of a less talented co-worker. We get easily frustrated in everyday traffic. We get upset when we are served a poor meal at a restaurant (or at home). Afterward, we tend to minimize and even forget our reactions to such "pinpricks," but added together they make up a life of pride that leads to self-centeredness, not one of humility that leads to holiness. Serious Christians can say with all sincerity, "I would die for you Lord," but will not stand for being inconvenienced for Him. Rather than desire the sufferings that others have endured, we must work to accept our personal sufferings — no matter how large or small they may be — as gifts from a loving Father who wants us to grow more like His beloved Son Jesus.

Recognition of our divine filiation is the bridge to sanctification and holiness. By embracing God as our loving Father, we can be as children in His loving arms, accepting anything that comes to us as a gift and making it a means to become more and more like His eternal Son, Jesus Christ.

Read

Read the chapters "Spiritual Childhood" and "Life of Childhood" in *The Way* (available free online at https://www.escrivaworks.org).

Meditate

Meditate on the following:

> *"Way of childhood. Abandonment. Spiritual infancy. All this is not utter nonsense, but a sturdy and solid Christian life."*[28]

- How is being a child "sturdy and solid"?
- Where in my life do I resist abandoning myself to God?

Pray

- Ask for the grace to see God always as a loving Father.
- Pray that all Christians might embrace the way of spiritual childhood.

Contemplate

How are we "sons in the Son"?

[28] Escrivá, *The Way*, 853.

Chapter 4

Free to Love

Freedom. It would be difficult to find a more powerful word in the modern lexicon. In America especially, we exalt freedom as the ultimate right; we are free to choose where to live, what career to pursue, and whom to marry. This freedom, we believe, is absolute: anything or anybody who appears to restrict our freedom is reviled as a threat to all that is good. In recent years, militant secularists have claimed that one of the most oppressive forces against freedom is religion. Religion means restrictions and rules, and therefore is opposed to freedom. The way to be truly free, so this thought goes, is to be free of the shackles of any restrictions on our choices.

St. Josemaría Escrivá lived in this modern age and witnessed the elevation of "freedom" to idolatrous status. He, too, highly valued freedom, but he had an altogether different concept of it than most modern men. He saw freedom as an essential part of the Christian pilgrimage to holiness, believing that freedom is not something granted by human authority, but rather flows from divine sonship. In this, he was in one accord with St. Paul, who wrote, "Through God you are no longer a slave but a son, and if a son then an heir" (Gal. 4:7). The Apostle to the Gentiles is telling the Galatians that ultimately there are two options open to each man: be either a slave or a son. Reject God and you are a slave: to your passions, to this

world, and to the devil. Follow God and you are a child of the Most
High God. Freedom and divine sonship are thus integrally linked,
and together form the bedrock on which personal sanctity rests.

Created Free

The exercise of freedom consists of two elements. The first is having
the ability to make a choice—free will. The second element is the
exercise of that ability—making a decision for one particular course
of action. Although the concept of free will has been studied and
debated by theologians for centuries, most people accept it as a fore-
gone conclusion. But what a marvelous thing that God granted the
human race free will! St. Josemaría loved to repeat the words of St.
Augustine, "God who created you without you, will not save you
without you." God could have created man in such a way that he
would have been impelled to love and follow Him. Instead He gave
man a profound choice—to willingly love God or to reject God's
love. The animals do not have this great privilege, only man. St.
Thomas Aquinas declared, "Men's supreme dignity lies in this, that
they are directed towards the good by themselves, and not by others."[29]

We can see illustrations of this wonderful and terrible gift
throughout Sacred Scripture. When God chose to become man in
order to save us, He left His fate in the hands of a teenage peasant
girl. Mary, when told that by her leave she would be the mother of
the Son of God, responded simply, "Let it be to me according to
your word" (Luke 1:38). Through one woman's free choice—a fiat
willingly given—God was able to undo the damage caused by the
first woman's free choice against him.

[29] St. Thomas Aquinas, *Super Epistolas S. Pauli lectura, Ad Romanos* II,
lect. III, in *Friends of God* by Josemaría Escrivá (New York, Scepter
Publishers, 2002), 48.

The ministry of Jesus also shows the great respect He has for the freedom of man. He says to the rich young man, "If *you wish* to be perfect, go, sell what you have and give to [the] poor, and you will have treasure in heaven. Then come, follow me" (Matt. 19:21, NAB, emphasis added), thus leaving it to the young man to decide whether to follow Christ or to continue to be enslaved by his possessions. Scripture tells us that the young man chose to turn away from Christ rather than give up his great wealth. In the end, this man freely chose slavery over freedom in Christ—and Christ accepted that disastrous choice out of his complete respect for the man's freedom.

The young man's decision demonstrates the irony of freedom: it is only by choosing to follow another that one can be truly free. This man chose to "follow his own way," which many would equate with freedom, but, in fact, his choice was one of slavery to the things of this world. The reality is that no matter what we choose to do with our lives, we will always be serving someone or something.

It is quite evident, as we can see in ourselves and in others, that everybody is a slave in some form or other. Some stoop before riches; others worship power; some, the relative tranquility of skepticism, and there are those who discover in sensuality their golden calf. The same happens in noble things. We put effort into a job of work, into an undertaking, large or small, into scientific, artistic, literary or spiritual activities. Wherever there is commitment and real passion, the person involved lives enslaved, joyfully devoting himself to fulfilling his task. We will be slaves either way. Since we must serve anyway, for whether we like it or not this is our lot as men, then there is nothing better than recognizing that Love has made us slaves of God. From the moment we recognize this we cease being slaves and become friends, sons.[30]

By choosing to be a slave of God, we become a son. Thus we see the second element of freedom: we are called to exercise our freedom to choose the good, which ultimately is always God. Making a choice that goes against the will of God is not a use of freedom, but the abuse of it. "Freedom finds its true meaning when it is put to the service of the truth which redeems, when it is spent in seeking God's infinite Love which liberates us from all forms of slavery."[31] Freedom that is disconnected from the good is simply license, which is the foundation of all sin: "Non serviam!" — "I will not serve," spoke the Evil One. God, in giving mankind the great gift of freedom, intended it to be used for one thing: to freely choose the good. "Reject the deception of those who appease themselves with the pathetic cry of 'Freedom! Freedom!' Their cry often masks a tragic enslavement, because choices that prefer error do not liberate. Christ alone sets us free, for He alone is the Way, the Truth, and the Life."[32]

Limits Lead to Freedom

One might object: If we are to submit ourselves to God, how can we say that this is freedom, since submission always means a restriction of our will? First we must recall that restrictions are not necessarily opposed to freedom. Imagine a society without any traffic laws. You can drive on either side of the road, there are no speed limits and no traffic signs or stop lights. One can easily see how

---

[30] Escrivá, *Friends of God* (New York, Scepter Publishers, 2002), 34–35.

[31] Ibid., 27.

[32] Ibid., 26.

this would quickly lead to dangerous chaos. Simply driving to the grocery store would be terrifying, and most people would choose to avoid the roads altogether—in other words, they would feel impelled to greatly restrict their movement. Yet by putting a few restrictions in place, traffic laws make driving a freeing experience: now you can easily get to where you want whenever you want without constant fear of an accident. Those traffic restrictions led to a real freedom.

Likewise in the spiritual life: by following the "restrictions" that God has placed upon us, we become free to follow Him. The married couple who eschews artificial birth control is free to accept the gift of children that God has planned for them. The man who fulfills the obligation to go to Mass each Sunday opens himself up to God's abundant graces available there. And the woman who faithfully gives away a portion of her income each month escapes from the slavery that attachment to money so quickly brings. By "restricting" ourselves, we give God permission to work in our lives and to deepen our connection to Him.

Following the "restrictions" of God often leads to great blessings in our lives. After my wife suffered three second-trimester miscarriages in succession, we were advised that "nothing can be done. It might be better to avoid pregnancy in the future." But we felt that we did not have a serious reason to do so, so we continued to be completely open to new life. We knew that God would take care of us in any situation, and we hoped for a miracle. Two years after that third miscarriage, we welcomed a healthy baby girl into our family. We "restricted" ourselves to following the Church's teachings regarding life and sexuality, and were thereby freed to accept from God's merciful hands a beautiful new life.

Because our spiritual DNA predicates fulfillment and true joy in union with God, the freedom we are given as sons of God is ultimately a freedom to pursue holiness. Any use of our freedom that moves us away from God, then, is an abuse of that freedom. If a carpenter were to use his tools in a way they were not intended to be used—a pencil as a cutting tool, for example—he would only be frustrated in his work. But by using each instrument as it is intended, he is able to accomplish the purpose of his work. Each person can only find contentment and peace in his spiritual life by being used by God as He intended him to be used. "Freedom is used properly when it is directed toward the good; and … it is misused when men are forgetful and turn away from the Love of loves. Personal freedom, which I defend and will always defend with all my strength, leads me to ask with deep conviction, though I am well aware of my own weakness: 'What do you want from me, Lord, so that I may freely do it?' "[33]

Another restriction that actually leads to freedom flows from the classic spiritual advice to "avoid the near occasion of sin." We are all fallen creatures, and as such we are all open to dangerous behavior and addictions. Avoiding even the temptations that lead to our most prevalent sins is a way to practice freedom. For who is more free—the alcoholic who avoids all bars or the one who frequents them each week? The addict is the slave, and in some sense or another, we are all addicted to sin. We are not just to avoid sin but also to avoid, as much as possible, anything that might tempt us to sin. By restricting ourselves we are free to live lives of holiness.

Many Paths to Holiness

Our freedom as God's children also includes each person's autonomy in discovering his own unique path to holiness. St. Paul wrote that

[33] Ibid.

> [Christ's] gifts were that some should be apostles, some
> prophets, some evangelists, some pastors and teachers, to
> equip the saints for the work of ministry, for building up the
> body of Christ, until we all attain to the unity of the faith and
> of the knowledge of the Son of God, to mature manhood, to
> the measure of the stature of the fulness of Christ; so that we
> may no longer be children, tossed to and fro and carried about
> with every wind of doctrine, by the cunning of men, by their
> craftiness in deceitful wiles. (Eph. 4:11–14)

In the Body of Christ, we are all different and unique members.
Some are called to be priests, some members of religious societies,
and most are called to be laypeople in the world. In that vast array
of lay faithful, each person has his own unique path to God. Surely
each path has its similarities to the others: we all need to pray and
depend on the sacraments for grace, of course. But the means by
which we deepen our walk with God are shaped by our individual
traits and characteristics. Through prayer, each person will unearth
his own way of communion with God:

> There are countless ways of praying, as I have already told
> you. We children of God don't need a method, an artifi-
> cial system, to talk with our Father. Love is inventive, full
> of initiative. If we truly love, we will discover our own
> intimate paths to lead us to a continuous conversation
> with Our Lord.[34]

The Church over the centuries has endorsed countless good
and holy devotions—the Rosary, the Way of the Cross, the Jesus
Prayer, to name a few—and only the arrogant would spurn these

---

[34] Escrivá, *Friends of God,* 255.

means flippantly. All of them can be used fruitfully to draw us closer to Christ and His Church. But none of these devotions are solely necessary for salvation and sanctification. I once knew a good, holy priest who confided to me that he did not pray the Rosary—that particular devotion was a struggle for him. Knowing the power of the Rosary, he recommended it to many people, but in his personal prayer life he put it aside in favor of other Marian devotions and prayers. While we must all follow the means of salvation put in place by Christ, such as the sacraments, each person must freely determine from the rich treasury of the Church the devotions that will strengthen his faith.

The rich diversity of its prayers and spiritualities is one of the beauties of the Catholic Faith, but it can also present a challenge. If we embrace a certain spirituality, say Franciscan or Ignatian, we can be tempted to see it as the only valid or the best spirituality for everyone. Or if we prefer a specific style of liturgy, the temptation is to condemn every other form. Throughout its history, though, the Church has embraced a wide array of worship styles and spiritualities, and each person has freedom to adapt his own spiritual practices—within Church guidelines—as best suits him.

"The Truth Will Make You Free"

Christ said "the truth will make you free" (John 8:32). Truth is an essential ingredient of freedom. Imagine a young man who decides to go out on his own, determined to make his way in New York City. Now imagine that he lives in Nebraska and has no idea how to reach the Big Apple. He drives around the country, going west, north, south, and east all in a vain attempt to reach his destination. He is free in the sense that no one will restrict his movements, but his ignorance of geography traps him in a fruitless attempt to reach his goal.

Our spiritual journeys have a destination as well, which is Heaven. Yet how many people try to reach that goal without knowing the way? When we make choices out of ignorance or, even worse, out of a rejection of the truth, we are not making a fully free choice, because we are limited by our false view of the world.

One of the surest ways to restrict our freedom is through self-deception. Perhaps we have a persistent sin that we have justified for years. This sin drags on our ability to fully serve God, yet we tell ourselves that it is not that bad or even harmless. It could be as small as impatience while driving or a habit of gossiping, or as serious as an addiction to pornography. Or perhaps it is not even a sin—perhaps we just underestimate our natural abilities, and by doing so deny ourselves the opportunity to be of greater service to the Church. An accurate view of reality frees us to follow God as He desires.

Free to Surrender

Freedom, it is important to remember, is a means to reach our final goal; it is not the goal itself. The person who worships at the altar of freedom ultimately engages in self-worship and lives in slavery to his passions and desires. Of course, the most obvious abuse of freedom today at the altar of self is the so-called "freedom to choose" abortion. No one has the freedom to kill an innocent child in the womb. A self-centered exaltation of freedom can also appear in more subtle forms that can impact even those who strive for holiness. Do we sacrifice our own free time in order to spend time with our children? Are we willing to give up certain personal freedoms in order to care for our aging parents? Whenever we choose self over others, we abuse our freedom.

So what is freedom's true goal? Paradoxically, it is self-surrender. On the surface, freedom and self-surrender appear to be at cross-purposes: Doesn't surrender mean that you are no longer free? Aren't you now a prisoner? As is often the case in the Christian life, what appears on the surface as a contradiction is actually an unveiling of a deeper reality.

We were made to be children of the Most High God, and, as we have noted, when we try to usurp His authority in our lives we enslave ourselves. Only when we use our freedom to surrender to God's Fatherhood are we free to fulfill our vocations.

> It is utterly false to oppose freedom and self-surrender, because self-surrender is a consequence of freedom. Look, when a mother sacrifices herself for love of her children, she has made a choice, and the more she loves the greater will be her freedom. If her love is great, her freedom will bear much fruit. Her children's good derives from her blessed freedom, which presupposes self-surrender, and from her blessed self-surrender, which is precisely freedom.[35]

Contrary to modern notions of freedom, true freedom leads to loving service: service to God and service to others. The preeminent example of this is the celibacy required of priests in the Latin Rite and members of religious orders. By sacrificing the good of married sexuality, celibate members of the Church are free to serve God and others with their whole lives.

Christ's own sacrifice on the Cross is the greatest act of freedom in history: "I lay down my life, that I may take it again. No one takes it from me, but I lay it down of my own accord. I have power to lay it down, and I have power to take it again; this charge I have received from my Father" (John 10:17–18). Christ is omnipotent and eternal, yet He chooses to submit Himself to the will of His Father, and emphasizes for all His followers His freedom in doing so.

---

[35] Escrivá, *Friends of God*, 30.

John's Gospel returns many times to this theme of freedom. Jesus willingly chose death at the hands of His enemies for our salvation, even though He could have easily escaped such a fate. Christ, as the divine Son of God, had complete freedom, and He used that freedom for self-surrender. This is the goal of the freedom given to us by God as well. By laying down our lives of our own free will, we will, like Jesus, be raised up in glory with the Father.

Free to Start Anew

Tradition says that when the angels were created they were given, with perfect knowledge of the consequences, a choice either to serve God or reject Him. The fallen angels—led by Lucifer—decided to reject God and spend eternity in Hell. Their choice was permanent—because of the nature of angels they are unable to change their decision. However, it is important to remember that man's choices, unlike the angels, are not permanent in this life—and this impermanence can be both a blessing and a curse. Reflect on the lives—and free choices—of the two apostles Judas and Peter. Both elected to reject Jesus at crucial times in their lives, thus choosing slavery over sonship. Judas remained in slavery all the way until the end, a slavery that eventually took his life. Peter, however, repented and thus broke the bonds of slavery, living again as a son of the Most High God.

Nothing is sadder than the person who is enslaved to his past. Whether the fall was great or small, sometimes we cannot overcome our mistakes. Perhaps we are estranged from a family member for a long-ago offense, or maybe we relive—over and over—some humiliating experience from years gone by. In any case, we do not freely live for God today, but are enslaved in reliving our past hurts. The redemption of St. Peter should be our model—we are always free to start a new life with God, no matter what our past may hold.

A certain freedom, in other words, always remains with us, even when we choose slavery to our passions and sins. It is a merciful freedom, one that offers us the chance to turn again to the Father and live as His sons. But it can also be one that condemns us, for until our deaths we retain the ability to choose self over God. Thus each day presents a fundamental choice: Will I serve my Lord and King in furthering His kingdom in my life and the lives of others, or will I enslave myself more and more to the enemy of all mankind?

> Love of God marks out the way of truth, justice, and goodness. When we make up our minds to tell Our Lord, 'I put my freedom in your hands,' we find ourselves loosed from the many chains that were binding us to insignificant things, ridiculous cares or petty ambitions. Then our freedom, which is a treasure beyond price, a wonderful pearl that it would be a tragedy to cast before swine, will be used by us entirely to learn how to do good.

This is the glorious freedom of the children of God.[36]

---

[36] Escrivá, *Friends of God*, 38.

READ

Read the chapter "Freedom, a Gift from God" in *Friends of God* (available free online at https://www.escriva-works.org).

MEDITATE

Meditate on the saying of St. Augustine:

> *"God, who created you without you,*
> *will not save you without you."*

- How does the awesome responsibility of freedom change how I look at my daily decisions?
- How have I abused my freedom?

PRAY

- Ask for the strength to direct your freedom to the good.
- Thank the Lord for the wonderful gift of your freedom as a son or daughter of God.

CONTEMPLATE

Consider the difference between the absolute freedom of God and our dependent freedom.

Chapter 5

Ambitious for Holiness

In the 1980s, a well-known movie popularized the phrase, "Greed is good." This saying encapsulated the stereotype of the corporate world: each person must ambitiously put his own desires and interests first, even if it means crushing any competitors. Although some people would argue that this phenomenon was peculiar to the '80s, every age of man has seen businessmen and women who place their own interests above any and all other considerations. There are countless colorful descriptions of this reality — "rat race," "dog-eat-dog," and "cutthroat" are just a few examples. All of them point to the idea that one must do anything he can to put himself on top. In ancient days, it was usually lineage that determined who was the upper class of society; today it is more of a social Darwinism whereby those are willing to do anything to succeed, no matter the cost or the morality, are catapulted to the upper echelons. In our culture, ambition breeds success, and ambition means promoting yourself relentlessly so that you can get ahead. The very idea of thinking of the good of another person over your own desires is perceived as a weakness and a sure path to failure.

Clearly, the Catholic who desires holiness can see the importance of avoiding this kind of selfish ambition. Such a lifestyle destroys any possibility of serving God and our neighbor. But perhaps surprisingly, St.

Josemaría did not reject ambition per se, and in fact embraced a certain form of ambition. He believed that every follower of Christ should have "holy ambition"—a driving desire to live completely for God, making every action an offering to God with the goal of becoming a saint.

Like someone with selfish ambition, a person with "holy ambition" strives with every fiber of his being to accomplish his goals. His focus is laser-like, and great personal sacrifices are as nothing to him if they help him get what he wants. The difference between selfish ambition and holy ambition is the final goal. For the former, it is a goal focused on self and this-worldly success. Holy ambition's goal of sanctity, on the other hand, focuses on God and otherworldly reward.

Those who have holy ambition will seek excellence in all their work, fight against lukewarmness, and strive to avoid even the taint of sin. We find the fundamental principle behind this ambition in these words of Christ, "the last will be first, and the first last" (Matt. 20:16). In other words, the ambitious Christians are those who put God and others first in their lives, instead of self. By doing so, they will "succeed" in the spiritual life.

Zeal for your House Consumes Me

Holiness and ambition might seem to conflict with each other. Isn't holiness a passive affair that is primarily for those who are meek and mild? But true sanctity is not for the faint of heart; it is for the one who faces up to numberless trials and frequent failures to stay the course laid out by Christ. St. Paul's zeal drove him to preach the Gospel to the ends of the known world, but he encountered obstacle after obstacle as he pursued his goal. He tells the Corinthians:

> Five times I have received at the hands of the Jews the forty lashes less one. Three times I have been beaten with rods; once I was stoned. Three times I have been

shipwrecked; a night and a day I have been adrift at sea; on frequent journeys, in danger from rivers, danger from robbers, danger from my own people, danger from Gentiles, danger in the city, danger in the wilderness, danger at sea, danger from false brethren; in toil and hardship, through many a sleepless night, in hunger and thirst, often without food, in cold and exposure. And, apart from other things, there is the daily pressure upon me of my anxiety for all the churches. (2 Cor. 11:24–28)

St. Francis Xavier traveled thousands of miles and punished his body relentlessly in order to bring the good news of Jesus Christ to the peoples of Asia. He overcame seemingly insurmountable obstacles in his single-minded devotion to following God's will for his life. This is the stuff of a saint: courage in the face of a world that oftentimes hates you.

In fact, when the Church canonizes a person, it says that he practiced "heroic virtue," for true sanctity is always heroic. Our fallen natures constantly prod us to choose the easier path, the one that leads to destruction. We are content to just "get by," rationalizing that God does not expect us to do things humanly impossible. God would never call my family to overseas missions, would He? He would never expect us to take in our elderly parents, would He? Too often, we fear being seen as a "fanatic" — one of the worst insults of the modern age. But only the person who is doggedly committed to holiness will ever achieve it.

St. Paul referred to the spiritual life as a race, and we can even compare it to a marathon — we do not follow Christ for a short spurt, but instead must dedicate our entire lives to Him. As an eager young convert, I was told by a mentor, "Slow down! You're going to burn out!" This can be wise advice, but it can also be used to excuse a halfhearted effort to follow the Lord. We temper our enthusiasm for the Faith by convincing ourselves that the "mature" way to be a disciple is "slow and steady." We avoid any extravagant displays of our faith, telling ourselves that we are just avoiding getting run down. But we have no idea when the time will come for us to stand before our Lord and Judge: it might be sixty years from now or it might be today. Although the spiritual life can be a marathon in length, we must run it like a sprint, trusting that God gives us the supernatural grace to follow Him unreservedly every day.

It is important to note that heroic virtue is not limited to the famous missionaries and leaders of the Church. Through the centuries countless men and women have sacrificed everything to follow the call of the Lord in unknown circumstances. How many mothers have given up comfort and worldly success in care of their children, sacrificing everything for the good of others? How many fathers have worked multiple jobs just to support the needs of their family? Not all saints are canonized, after all.

My own father-in-law was one of those "unknown" saints. His father, a police officer, died in the line of duty when my father-in-law had just finished high school. He did not look upon such a hardship with self-pity, but instead determined to persevere in his Catholic Faith and later raise his own family in the Church. Although he did not always agree with the many changes that were occurring in the Church in the 1960s and 1970s, he never once considered the possibility of abandoning the faith of his youth. Instead, he quietly strove on, living a virtuous life, praying the Rosary daily, and attending Mass faithfully. Even in the face of debilitating illness in his final years, he pressed on. No one would call my father-in-law "ambitious" — he was a quiet, gentle soul — but that is, in fact, what he was: ambitious in serving God as his state in life required. How many men and women like this have lived throughout the centuries?

The fact that sanctity can only be achieved through hard work and perseverance should not surprise us—these qualities are necessary to accomplish any worthwhile earthly goal, and the heavenly goal of holiness is no different. We only achieve it by way of a constant, lifelong battle. C. S. Lewis once gave the analogy that Christ resisting sin throughout his life was like one man standing up to the entire Nazi German army. Because of our fallen natures, every day is a ferocious battle with sin and weakness, the winning of which demands fortitude and courage. These battles may not on the surface appear heroic, but simply resisting the urge to snap at your annoying co-worker can require every bit of grace and strength available to you. These little victories make up the foundation of a life of sanctity. The weak person, however, gives in to these passions and gives them control over his life. Christ Himself praised the spiritually ambitious. In the Parable of the Talents (Matt. 25:14–30), Christ commends those who ambitiously seek to multiply their gifts—the person who timidly hides his talent is condemned. It is only the one who uses his talents to serve God and help others who is greatly rewarded. Likewise, St. Paul writes to the Corinthians, "Run so as to win. Every athlete exercises discipline in every way. They do it to win a perishable crown, but we an imperishable one. Thus I do not run aimlessly; I do not fight as if I were shadowboxing. No, I drive my body and train it" (1 Cor. 9:24–27, NAB). The Christian life is not for the faint-hearted; it is for those who want to pursue holiness with all of their heart, mind, and soul. We are to "run as to win," knowing the great prize that awaits us at the end.

One other significant difference between selfish ambition and holy ambition we must also recognize. Selfish ambition is obsessed with "greatness," and this greatness is measured by an action's outward impact on the world. So those who are ambitious for the things of this world want to build the highest skyscraper or own the home everyone envies or have the best wardrobe of stylish clothes. But for the spiritually ambitious, it is the little things that matter—those actions that no one sees except God. The focus of the spiritually ambitious is not the cover of national magazines or praise from television talking heads—it is making choices that lead us to God.

Practically, this means that not everyone needs to go out and preach like St. Paul, found an order to help the poor like Mother Teresa, or lead the Church like St. Leo the Great. Some are called to such great works, but most are not. However, every follower of Christ is called to ambitiously pursue holiness in each and every activity of life, whether great or small. Again, there is an irony here: worldly ambition looks at the big things of life: being the head of a company, having a mansion and a new large TV. But holy ambition does the opposite—it looks to the little things of life: changing diapers without complaint, helping a friend in need without fanfare, visiting a nursing home.

The "little way" of St. Thérèse, so beloved by St. Josemaría, emphasized the importance of making every action, no matter how seemingly inconsequential, one done in love. Holiness is not to be equated with great outward deeds—although some may be called to those—but instead, as Mother Teresa once said, little deeds done with great love. If you look back at the Parable of the Talents, you see that one man produced five talents and another only two, yet both were praised equally. It is not the results that Christ praises, but the loving—and ambitious—use of the talents we are given.

For example, I know a mother who makes designs with the food on her children's lunch plates just to communicate her love and to brighten their day. Sure, just tossing them a sandwich would fulfill her duties, but holiness seeks to go beyond what is required. Looking back at several experiences with loved ones' hospital stays, I am always struck by the enormous impact a loving nurse has—versus the one who is clearly there just to punch the clock. The former allows God's love to radiate through her care for others. These are not works that will make the front page of any papers, but they are ones that are surely noticed in Heaven.

The story of Cain and Abel is instructive for us here. Genesis 4 tells us that Cain "brought an offering of the fruit of the ground" as an offering to the Lord (Gen. 4:3), whereas Abel "brought the firstlings of his flock" (Gen. 4:4). In other words, Abel offered the best portion of his work to the Lord, while Cain was content just to offer anything he could find. In response, God looked with favor on Abel's sacrifice but not on Cain's. Did God need the best in order to survive? Was He angry because He liked only the richest produce and fattest calves? Of course not. God, who gave man his very existence as an outpouring of His divine love, calls man to offer himself back to God in love. Only by doing so will man find joy and peace. God desires that each person carry out each and every thing with love and devotion, making every action a fragrant offering to Him.

Excellence in All Things

Imagine that nurse who loves her work and truly cares for her patients. She wants to help each and every one of them to recover and to experience God's love during their convalescence. But what if she did her work tasks with little effort and half-heartedly—being sloppy about dispensing medicine and not being careful to follow the doctor's exact instructions? Would such actions reflect a soul that wants to glorify God in all things?

An important component of holy ambition is the desire to do every task to the best of our abilities. The spiritual life does not only consist of our prayer life and outward works of charity; it consists of the totality of our lives. St. Josemaría loved to quote Mark 7:37, where the people say of Jesus, "He has done all things well." What particularly interested St. Josemaría was the word "all"—over and over the Spanish saint emphasized that the work of redemption was not confined merely to Christ's passion or even to His three years of public ministry. Instead, St. Josemaría insisted that the entirety of Christ's life—from His conception in His mother's womb to His ascension to His heavenly father—was redemptive. In other words, even when Christ was doing carpentry work for a neighbor, this work He offered to the Father for our salvation.

As followers of Christ, we join in that redemption by our own work. Should that work then be sloppy and poorly done? Or should it be done with care and excellence? St. Josemaría recalls going to a cathedral with a few young men and pointing out the craftsmanship of the towers, even in parts that could not be easily seen. "I ... pointed out that none of the beauty of this work could be seen from below. To give them a material lesson in what I had been previously explaining to them, I would say, 'This is God's work, this is working for God! To finish your personal work perfectly, with all the beauty and exquisite refinement of this tracery stonework.' Seeing it, my companion would understand that all the work we had seen was a prayer, a loving dialogue with God."[37] If a person does his work in a slapdash way, he is not offering his "first-fruits" to God, but instead serving as idols his own comfort and pleasure.

St. Josemaría alludes in his anecdote to our toughest challenge: doing our best in those jobs that no one else notices. Instead of imitating the cathedral worker, we can be tempted to let our work slide when it will go unnoticed by others. My early training as a computer programmer included learning to write comments in my code—notes that would mostly go unseen, but might eventually guide another programmer making changes to my software. How

[37] Escrivá, *Friends of God,* 65.

tempting it became to write just a few cursory words—after all, there was a good chance no one would ever read them. Or a janitor might quickly clean the back of a closet, assuming that no one will ever inspect that area of his work. But God sees all. He desires that everything we do be done with enthusiasm and love. Even a child can be taught to make his bed with thoroughness so that he sees the value of offering his best for God in every situation.

Fighting Lukewarmness

One of the sad realities of history is that only a small percentage of the members of the Church live saintly lives. In many cases, a lack of holiness is due to a lack of desire for holiness—people are not ambitious for sanctity. But it is also true that many who aspire for holiness also fail to reach their goal. Obviously, God wants them to be holy, so why doesn't it happen? Lukewarmness—the great enemy of holy ambition. "Fight against that weakness which makes you lazy and careless in your spiritual life. Remember that it might well be the beginning of lukewarmness."[38] Lukewarmness is that attitude that our Lord condemned in the church at Laodicea: "I know your works: you are neither cold nor hot. Would that you were cold or hot! So, because you are lukewarm, and neither cold nor hot, I will spew you out of my mouth" (Rev. 11:15–16). We can also hear Christ warning against lukewarmness in the Parable of the Sower:

> A sower went out to sow his seed; and as he sowed, some
> fell along the path, and was trodden under foot, and the
> birds of the air devoured it. And some fell on the rock;
> and as it grew up, it withered away, because it had no

---

[38] Escrivá, *The Way*, number 325.

moisture. And some fell among thorns; and the thorns grew with it and choked it. And some fell into good soil and grew, and yielded a hundredfold. (Luke 8:5–8)

The seed of the Word can easily be choked among the weeds of life, and lukewarmness can be the primary cause of such a perilous scenario. Why is lukewarmness so dangerous? The one who is lukewarm allows the cares of this world to dominate his thoughts and overwhelm his spiritual life; since he is lukewarm about spiritual concerns, he pushes aside any attempts to grow in holiness as extraneous activities.

If I desire to become an Olympian, nothing could be more detrimental in my quest than a feeling of malaise toward the necessary training. The phrase "laid-back Olympian" is an oxymoron. Is not the same true in the quest to become a spiritual Olympian? One who is lukewarm treats spiritual activities such as prayer, living the virtues, and receiving the sacraments with apathy and coldness. Such a person might continue with these activities for a time, but only out of a sense of habit or obligation. No burning fire within drives him to strive for the perfection Christ sets as the goal. "It hurts me to see the danger of lukewarmness in which you place yourself when you do not strive seriously for perfection in your state in life. Say with me: I don't want to be lukewarm! *Confige timore tuo carnes meas*, pierce thou my flesh with thy fear: grant me, my God, a filial fear that will make me react!"[39] Lukewarmness is wholly opposed to holy ambition and quickly leads one to spiritual apathy and even spiritual death.

We all know people who have had extreme conversion experiences because of which their lives change overnight; they go

---

[39] Ibid., 326

from selfish, worldly individuals to ones wholly devoted to God. Unfortunately, we may have also seen some of these converts cool over time—the day-in and day-out of following Christ takes its toll, and the convert begins to slip in his practice of the faith. Even the most enthusiastic follower of Christ can fall into a rut. The temptations of this world are great, and they always pull us away from God. We come to accept and justify "little" sins—venial sins—as a natural part of who we are. But every sin is a great offense against God, and we must constantly strive to avoid all sin: "I already know that you avoid mortal sins. You want to be saved! But you are not worried by that constant and deliberate falling into venial sins, even though in each case you feel God's call to conquer yourself. It is your lukewarmness that gives you this bad will."[40]

Even a person who does not minimize the evil of venial sin can stop striving for greater and greater sanctity. "Small" sins can easily escape the notice of one who is not vigilant against them. For example, impatience at the little frustrations of life—burnt food, a long line at the store, or a difficult in-law—can be rationalized as justified in our specific situations. But such impatience masks a deeper sin of pride: the attitude that I don't "deserve" such hardships. Instead of taking these difficulties and offering them to God, we use them as a small means to exert our will over His. After all, by whose permission was the food burnt, the line long, or the in-law tedious?

If you are driving up a mountain, what will happen if you put the car in neutral? Of course, you will begin to slide back down. And the goal of holiness is a high mountain indeed, which we can only climb with the help of God's grace. Only by fostering holy ambition and fighting against lukewarmness will we even desire to reach the summit of that holy mountain. "You are lukewarm

---

[40] Ibid., 327

if you carry out lazily and reluctantly those things that have to do with our Lord; if deliberately or 'shrewdly' you look for some way of cutting down your duties; if you think only of yourself and of your comfort; if your conversations are idle and vain; if you do not abhor venial sin; if you act from human motives."[41]

Hating Sin

As mentioned already, a careless attitude toward venial sin is a dangerous consequence of lukewarmness. Do you treat "small" sins as a "minor" problem, or do you recognize that any sin—even the smallest one—is a greater calamity than the physical destruction of the world? Every sin is a rejection of our calling as children of a holy God, and so every sin should be a cause of great sorrow. Study the lives of the saints. Do you notice how harsh their self-assessment is? These very models of Christian living saw themselves as the worst of sinners. Were they deluded? No, it is the rest of us who are deluded—deluded into thinking that our sins are no big deal, becoming lukewarm to the reality of sin in our lives. The saints realize how evil each and every sin is, so they grieve mightily at any instance of sin in their own lives.

Hatred of sin is not equivalent to scrupulosity. We do not need to invent sins in our lives in order to feel guilty about our walk with God; actual sins we commit should convict us enough. However, sin becomes so familiar in our lives that we do not loathe and detest it as we should. Perhaps we exaggerate our accomplishments in front of others in order to puff ourselves up. Or we judge the actions of others in our workplace, assuming the worst of them. These "little" sins go unnoticed by the outside world, especially when they are part and parcel of what society considers "normal"—over-competitiveness,

[41] Ibid., 331

gossip, self-interest, pride. Over time they even go unnoticed by us. But they are the beginning cracks in the dam that will lead to a flood of more serious sins. Whenever we allow ourselves to be content with venial sins, we have begun down the path to mortal sin and spiritual death.

"Holy ambition" is, simply put, the desire to be holy. Or, as our Lord said, "love the Lord your God with all your heart, and with all your soul, and with all your strength, and with all your mind" (Luke 10:27). Every fiber of our being must be directed toward holiness—all our actions, our words, and even our thoughts. But how can we do this? What practical steps can we take so that each day we draw closer to God and become more like Him? Just as the Olympian develops a specific plan so that he might achieve his goal—the gold medal—so, too, must each Christian have a practical plan to achieve the goal of sanctity. St. Josemaría worked with laypeople for decades developing practical means to becoming holy, and to these we will turn next.

READ

Read the chapter "Lukewarmness" in *The Way* (available free online at https://www.escrivaworks.org).

MEDITATE

Meditate on the words of St. Paul:

> *"Run so as to win. Every athlete exercises discipline in every way. They do it to win a perishable crown, but we an imperishable one. Thus I do not run aimlessly; I do not fight as if I were shadowboxing. No, I drive my body and train it."*
> *(1 Cor. 9:24–27, NAB)*

- Do I strive to "win" in the battle for holiness?
- How do I lack discipline in my efforts for sanctity?

PRAY

- Ask God for the abiding desire to be saint.
- Pray for the holiness of all people.

CONTEMPLATE

How do we reconcile "holy ambition" with the command to die to self?

PART TWO

Building a Saintly Life

Chapter 6

Be a Contemplative in the Midst of the World

When a young man or woman has discerned a call to the religious life, one of the first things to be considered is what type of religious life will be chosen: contemplative or active? Contemplative orders typically spend a great deal of time in prayer; often cloistered, their primary focus is praying for the needs of the world. Active orders, on the other hand, are more directly devoted to works of charity outside the monastery or convent. These orders, of course, dedicate much time to prayer, but their mission is to perform some service for the Church or the world. Both types of orders have benefited the Church immensely over the centuries, and both have led many people to live lives of holiness.

Lay people, naturally, are not divided into two different groups. With various responsibilities, such as work and family, they are not able to devote many hours each day to prayer like the contemplative orders do. So it might be surprising that St. Josemaría loved to say that lay people are called to be "contemplatives in the midst of the world." He wrote, "The street does not get in the way of our contemplative life; the hubbub of the world is, for us, a place for prayer."[42] Even though most people

---

[42] Josemaría Escrivá, "Letter, Jan. 9, 1959," in *Holiness and the World,* (New York: Scepter Publishers, 1997), 101.

cannot lead what would traditionally be called a "contemplative" life, St. Josemaría was convinced nonetheless that every Christian is called to be a contemplative. Conversation with God was not something to be restricted to certain times and places, but was instead something that could—and should—be done anywhere and anytime.

Live a Life of Prayer

The fuel that powers a life of sanctity is the interior life—a life of prayer. It is simply not possible to work toward Christ's desire that we "be perfect" as our Father in Heaven is perfect (see Matt. 5:48) without a strong interior life. The Sermon on the Mount begins by describing what a life of holiness should look like, climaxing with the command to be perfect (see Matt. 5). But immediately following this description of a holy life, Christ details what the proper interior life looks like (see Matt. 6). He states, "But when you pray, go into your room and shut the door and pray to your Father who is in secret; and your Father who sees in secret will reward you" (Matt. 6:6), and "when you fast, do not look dismal, like the hypocrites, for they disfigure their faces that their fasting may be seen by men. Truly, I say to you, they have received their reward. But when you fast, anoint your head and wash your face, that your fasting may not be seen by men but by your Father who is in secret; and your Father who sees in secret will reward you" (Matt. 6:16–18). In other words, a relationship with God is primarily an interior one—it is not something we robe ourselves with for others to see, but an ever-unfolding friendship in the most intimate recesses of our heart. The deep wellspring born there will then overflow into all aspects of our life.

Christ Himself provides the model of the intimate prayer life necessary for holiness. In the Gospels we often see Him at prayer before His most significant tasks. Before Christ chose His apostles, he went out to pray (Luke 6:12–16). Before He gave His life for our salvation, He retreated to the Garden of Gethsemane in order to pour Himself out in prayer to His Father (see Luke 22:39–46). As Luke emphasizes, "Jesus often withdrew to lonely places and prayed" (Luke 5:16, NIV). And as this intimacy with the Father in prayer was necessary for Christ, our sonship with Him means it is also necessary for us. "The foundation of all we do as citizens — as Catholic citizens — lies in an intense interior life. It lies in being really and truly men and women who turn their day into an uninterrupted conversation with God."[43]

But how do we have a strong interior life — how do we build a life of prayer? Over the centuries, countless saints and teachers have given the Church ways of praying. Each of them is valuable, and each can lead one closer to God. Respecting each person's freedom, St. Josemaría did not institute a specific way of praying; instead, he left that up to each person to decide.

There are countless ways of praying, as I have already told you. We children of God don't need a method, an artificial system, to talk with our Father. Love is inventive, full of initiative. If we truly love, we will discover our own intimate paths to lead us to a continuous conversation with Our Lord.[44]

St. Josemaría did, however, suggest certain guidelines and activities — developed and refined over decades of spiritual direction — that his experience showed him were particularly useful for lay people seeking to be contemplatives in the midst of the world.

Recognize the Presence of God

The vital component to any life of prayer is that it must integrate naturally with one's lifestyle. A mother with several young children

---

[43] Escrivá, *The Forge*, 572.
[44] Escrivá, *Friends of God*, 255.

cannot live like a Trappist monk, nor can a CEO of a multinational corporation live as a member of a mendicant order. Each person has certain obligations in life, and abandoning them on the pretext of prayer does nothing to honor God. That CEO and that mother—and you and I—must see that God is right where we are. When we truly recognize the presence of God at all times and in all situations, then prayer becomes natural to the places of our daily lives, just as it seems natural to pray when we enter a church. "In our inner life, in our external behavior, in our dealings with others, in our work," St. Josemaría wrote,

> [E]ach of us must try to maintain a constant presence of God, conversing with him, carrying on a dialogue in a way that does not show outwardly. Or, rather, which as a rule does not express itself in audible words, but which certainly should show itself in the determination and loving care we put into carrying out all our duties, both great and small.[45]

Striving to recognize that God is always present, we will act differently:

> Children.... How they seek to behave worthily in the presence of their parents.
> And the children of kings, in the presence of their father the king, how they seek to uphold the royal dignity!
> And you?—Don't you realize that you are always in the presence of the great King, God, your Father?[46]

Each moment becomes an opportunity to be with the one who made us and loves us. This is not daydreaming or living some flight

---

[45] Ibid., 19.
[46] Escrivá, *The Way,* 265.

of fancy. It is the concrete realization that God is always with us and He wants to be involved in every aspect of our lives. Nothing can — or should — be hidden from Him. One of the greatest temptations for lay people in the midst of the world is to forget the sacred while immersed in the secular. Tight deadlines, constant stresses, and familial demands all barrage our minds throughout the day, making the presence of God seem far off indeed. But the reality is that God is truly present at each and every moment of the day, making every moment sacred.

The unending presence of God means that every action of each day can be holy — from writing an email to making spaghetti. But without at least brief times set aside just for prayer, it is too easy to lose sight of God's presence. So next we will consider St. Josemaría's specific advice for creating oases of prayer and contemplation in our daily lives.

Make a Plan of Life

Most of our major undertakings meet with more success if our first step is to make a plan. Over the years of his ministry, St. Josemaría developed a "Plan of Life" that he recommended — practical guidelines to help us win the battle for holiness. "You tell me: when the chance comes to do something big, then! ... Then? Are you seriously trying to convince me — and to convince yourself — that you will be able to win in the supernatural Olympics without daily preparation, without training?"[47] The Plan of Life is a tool for those who wish to develop their interior life, a battle plan in the struggle against sin and lukewarmness. Again, what the Spanish saint recommended was not a new spirituality, but instead a general framework that anyone can adapt to his specific situation.

---

[47] Escrivá, *The Way*, 822.

Our entire plan of life ... [is] designed for men and women who work in the midst of the world, carrying out ordinary everyday jobs. They are not rigid rules, which presuppose a life apart [from the world], but a flexible method, which has a wonderful capacity to adapt to any life of intense professional work, the way a rubber glove molds itself perfectly to the hand using it. In fact, our interior life (contemplative life, in all situations) avails itself of and is nourished by that external life of work proper to each of us.[48]

This plan includes daily, weekly, monthly, and other regular activities that help build a strong interior life and a recognition of the presence of God at all times.

Heroic Minute

Maintaining a disciplined plan of life is a daily battle, and many battles are won or lost in the first minutes. The Plan of Life, then, must begin in the first moments of each day. St. Josemaría liked to call the first minute of the day the "heroic minute," for it is the very first opportunity to overcome our weakness and offer the day to the Lord. "The heroic minute. It's time to get up, on the dot! Without hesitation, a supernatural thought and ... up! The heroic minute; here you have a mortification that strengthens your will and does not weaken your body."[49] St. Josemaría said he would often promise his body a nap later in the day if it got up in time in the morning (but would then skip that nap when the afternoon rolled around). By winning a little victory over the flesh to start the day, we will be better able to overcome the pull of the flesh during the rest of the day.

---

[48] Escrivá, "Letter, Oct. 15, 1948, no. 22," in *Opus Dei in the Church*, 197.
[49] Escrivá, *The Way*, 206.

Although having such a start to the day might seem a minor undertaking, it can actually be quite difficult in today's world. Previous generations were well-attuned to the natural rising and setting of the sun. A farmer's daily schedule was set by the rhythms of nature. This is not the case today. With the advent of electricity and artificial lighting, now we are able to retire or rise whenever we wish. For most people, this often means staying up late at night and then struggling to get out of bed in the morning. A key to success in having a "heroic minute" each morning is to have a "heroic minute" each night by retiring at a reasonable hour. Too often the reason we don't win the battle at the start of the day is because we succumbed to the temptation to watch just "one more show" the previous night. These mundane choices can have a significant impact on our spiritual life.

Morning Offering

The "heroic minute" is then to be followed by a morning offering, in which one offers the entire day — its joys, its sorrows, its gifts, and its challenges — for the glory of God. But more than anything, the morning offering is an opportunity to place ourselves in the service of God. A simple example of a morning offering is:

> I will serve you, God.
> O Jesus, I offer You my prayers, works, and sufferings of this day for all the intentions of Your Most Sacred Heart. Amen.[50]

By starting the day declaring *Serviam!* — *I will serve!* — we place all of our activities at God's feet, acknowledging that none of them should be for our glory, but for His. In suggesting a morning

---

[50] "Morning Offering," United States Conference of Catholic Bishops, accessed June 27, 2022, https://www.usccb.org/prayers/morning-offering/.

offering, St. Josemaría was following in the footsteps of a long line of spiritual directors and saints in the Catholic Church through the centuries. He knew that the rest of the plan would fall apart if it did not begin with the consecration of each day to God.

Mass

If the heroic minute and the morning offering are the beginnings of one's daily plan, the Mass is its central activity. St. Josemaría—like all the saints—had an abiding devotion to the Mass, and he frequently counseled that people try to attend daily if possible. The saint stated in a 1960 homily that "Holy Mass brings us face to face with one of the central mysteries of our faith, because it is the gift of the Blessed Trinity to the Church. It is because of this that we can consider the Mass as *the center and the source* of a Christian's spiritual life" (*Christ Is Passing By* 87, emphasis added). St. Josemaría's conviction about the central place of the Mass in the life of the Christian anticipated the declaration by Vatican II a few years later that the Eucharist is the "source and summit" of the Christian life.[51]

The Mass is primarily a means of encountering the Trinity: the Son offers Himself by the will of the Father and in cooperation with the Holy Spirit, and through this offering we enter into the very mystery of the Godhead.[52] As Christ offered up His whole earthly life—from His conception to His Ascension—to the Father in His Crucifixion, so we must offer up our lives to the Father. How exactly do we unite our sorrows, joys, sufferings, and victories to Christ's? The Mass. In God's merciful plan, He gives us a unique way to become one with Christ and His work of salvation. In the Mass, we are mystically transported to Calvary where the salvific

[51] *Lumen Gentium*, 11.
[52] Escrivá, *Christ is Passing By,* 86.

death of Christ is eternally present. Thus, all the activities of our day with all their pains and sorrows can be joined to Christ's redemptive sacrifice and offered to the Father for His glory. If what we seek is that our whole life be an offering to God, clearly the Mass truly is the central activity of our lives.

It would be amazing enough if we were just allowed access to the bounteous graces available by attending Mass. But God in His abundant love goes even further — He allows us to sacramentally receive the very Body and Blood of His son Jesus Christ! We can never receive our Lord too often, and in keeping with the direction of the Church since the time of Pope St. Pius X, St. Josemaría suggested that Catholics communicate daily if they were properly disposed (see *The Way,* 539). The Eucharist is the food that gives us strength, and just as we all need food each day to keep our physical strength, so do we need the Eucharist to keep our spiritual strength. The Plan of Life revolves around the reception of Communion at Mass, for without the graces that come from our Lord in the Eucharist, all our plans to follow Him are sure to fail.

We can never underestimate or take for granted the importance of grace for living a holy life. As Christ said to the rich young man, "No one is good but God alone" (Mark 10:18). Any good we do is always a result of grace, and so we must cling to the means God in His merciful love has given to us to obtain that grace — first and foremost, the sacraments. Regular reception of the Eucharist is vitally important to keep flowing a torrent of grace through each day of our lives.

Daily Spiritual Exercises

Although each day's spiritual center is the Mass, other daily spiritual practices are also important, such as praying the Angelus, praying the Rosary, and engaging in mental prayer.

These practices are useful to the ordinary Catholic living a busy life, as each of them are short activities (less than twenty minutes) that can be carried out at a variety of times and in a variety of places. Each of these practices, furthermore, reminds us of spiritual realities in the midst of our ordinary, earthly activities.

One of the challenges of keeping the Plan of Life is maintaining the discipline to actually practice its elements. It is all too common for people to begin saying the Rosary daily, for example, but then cease the practice soon after when the initial enthusiasm wavers. This is why St. Josemaría was always practical in his advice—make sure that you plan your spiritual activities around your responsibilities. And, do not attempt to force new activities into your schedule too quickly or haphazardly. Start simple. For example, say a chaplet while commuting, or say the Angelus in your office with the door closed at the beginning of a lunch break. Rather than trying to settle four young children for a Rosary before lunch, mom can pray the Angelus with them, which takes just a few minutes. At the end of the day, as she sits down to nurse her infant—a time when earthly anxieties seem to come rushing in—she can pray her Rosary. Sure, she might nod off, but as the psalmist says, God blesses His children while they sleep! Trying to start by committing to hours of new practices is a path sure to fail. Recognize what is possible and work within your own limitations.

Spiritual Reading

St. Jerome famously said, "Ignorance of Scripture is ignorance of Christ." The primary way we know about our Lord is through the Bible, especially the Gospels, and therefore another key feature of the Plan of Life is spiritual reading. The Christian's goal is to become as Christ-like as possible, and how can we become like someone we don't know? St. Josemaría recommended taking at least five to ten minutes every day to reflect on some scene in the Gospels, picturing oneself in that scene in order to meditate on Christ's actions more deeply (see *Friends of God*, 216). But simply reading the Gospels is not an end to itself; no, after reading about Christ, the Christian is then to model himself after the Lord in His own life. One of the first points for meditation in *The Way* states, "May your behavior and your conversation be such that everyone who sees or hears you can say: This man reads the life of Jesus Christ."[53] By spending time each day reading the life of Jesus, our lives, then, will "read" His life to others.

Over the centuries, the Church has developed a means for deep meditative reading of the Sacred Scriptures: *Lectio Divina* ("Divine Reading"). This method, which originated in the monasteries but is useful to anyone who wishes to apply the truths of Scripture to their lives, consists of four steps. Pope Benedict XVI, in his apostolic exhortation *Verbum Domini*, identified a question we can ask ourselves for each of these steps:

1. *Lectio* (Reading)—what does the biblical text say in itself?
2. *Meditatio* (Meditation)—what does the biblical text say to us?
3. *Oratio* (Prayer)—what do we say to the Lord in response to His word?
4. *Contemplatio* (Contemplation)—what conversion of mind, heart, and life is the Lord asking of us?[54]

The important thing to remember here is that reading the Bible is not like reading any other book—our encounter with Christ in

---

[53] Escrivá, *The Way*, 2.
[54] Benedict XVI, *Verbum Domini: Post-Synodal Apostolic Exhortation on the Word of God in the Life and Mission of the Church* (September 30, 2010), 87.

the Scriptures should transform us to become more Christ-like, allowing others to read Christ's life in our life.

One priest told me that he had been preaching *lectio divina* for some time with limited success. He found that this type of meditative reading seemed foreign to many of his listeners; the primary type of reading for many people is of the superficial sort — magazine articles and short online blurbs. Going deeply into a text was just too difficult. So he developed a few practical tips: (1) do your *lectio divina* in a quiet place with little or no distractions; (2) don't try to spend more than ten to fifteen minutes at first; and (3) start off every reading with a prayer to the Holy Spirit for help. Taking these small suggestions, many people were better able to engage the Sacred Text on a deeper, more profound level.

Mortification

In addition to the specific prayer practices in the Plan of Life, St. Josemaría also urged practicing mortifications throughout the day. To many, the term "mortifications" might seem to come from another age; it brings forth images of dark, medieval cells populated by monks whipping each other bloody. But mortifications are all those activities that help us to control our sinful impulses and desires. They can be as simple as denying ourselves a second helping at dinner, allowing others to speak first in conversations, or choosing the longer line at the checkout counter. At a time when voluntary mortifications were becoming less and less commonly practiced in the Church, St. Josemaría was a strong proponent of these traditional spiritual exercises. In fact, he saw them as essential to the spiritual life: "Unless you mortify yourself, you'll never be a prayerful soul."[55] Mortifications, in fact, are prayer: prayer of the senses (cf. *Christ Is Passing By* 78).

[55] Escrivá, *The Way*, 172.

Mortifications, of course, can be voluntary or involuntary. Each person is faced with little obstacles each day, such as heavy traffic or bad food, which he cannot control. Our response to these inconveniences help shape our quest for holiness: Do we accept them cheerfully and without complaint? Or do we become annoyed and increasingly bitter at such hardships? The saint faces all obstacles in life—both big and small—cheerfully and in union with the Passion of Christ.

But involuntary mortifications are only one part of the equation: all Christians should also choose to add small mortifications to their day, such as taking the less comfortable seat in a room, skipping desert after a meal or having only one cup of coffee. Such mortifications are simply the way we become spiritually strong:

> See how many sacrifices men and women make, willingly or less willingly, to take care of their bodies, protect their health, or gain the respect of others.... Are we unable to stir ourselves at the thought of the immensity of God's love, so poorly requited by men, and mortify what needs to be mortified so that our hearts and minds may be more attentive to our Lord?[56]

The model for mortifications is the life of Christ—from His humbling birth in a manger to the suffering on the Cross (cf. *Friends of God,* 128), He did not choose a path of ease and comfort, but a way of mortification and suffering. This is the way of God, and one does not come to Him except by that path.

Mortifications should not be done in a gloomy or a flashy way: "Choose mortifications that don't mortify others."[57] If fasting causes

---

[56] Escrivá, *Friends of God,* 135.
[57] Escrivá, *The Way,* 179.

you to become cranky with your kids in the evening, choose instead another sacrifice—such as eating food that you don't care for. Find mortifications that are spiritually beneficial, and then make a firm plan to carry them out. What they are matters less than sticking with them. Our mortifications should be taken on quietly and joyfully, for, like almost any human activity, mortifications can lead to pride; one must be on guard so that they remain a humble path to holiness. All mortifications should be united to Christ's supreme mortification of becoming man and dying for us. With this attitude, we will have joy in our self-denial, for what a great privilege to be sharing in God's great act of salvation!

Examination of Conscience

Just as it is important to begin every day ready for battle, so it is just as vital to end each day reviewing our successes and failures. At the close of each day we should make an examination of conscience, specifically looking at where we have failed to live up to the Christian ideal. This is not to be a general examination of one's whole life, or an in-depth one like that done before going to Confession—it should focus only on one or two areas of struggle. By reviewing the day—and looking toward the next—we can gauge our progress in the spiritual life and beg for forgiveness for the times we fell, trusting in God's infinite mercy to pick us back up again.

Why during our examination of conscience should we also be preparing for the next day? We all have specific areas of weakness and failure in our lives, and the exam is a moment not only to acknowledge these, but also to resolve to overcome them in the future. If my particular area of weakness right now is impatience with my children, and I see that I failed to resist this weakness several times today, I need to make a concrete plan that will help me succeed tomorrow. Do I avoid a particular co-worker? I might resolve to keep in mind that he is made in the image of God. Am I lazy at work, rather than diligent in my duties? I can develop a specific schedule for completing tasks, with rewards for accomplishing them. In these ways, we can truly progress in overcoming our persistent weaknesses and sins.

Other Regular Activities

The core of the Plan of Life involves many daily activities, but St. Josemaría also suggested certain spiritual practices at other regular intervals. These include: regular visits to the tabernacle to meet our Lord in the Blessed Sacrament; regular, even weekly, Confession; and annual weekend retreats.

Adoration of the Blessed Sacrament is one of the great gifts of the Church. What a privilege it is to be in the very presence of the Lord! Jesus Christ, truly present in the Eucharist, is waiting for us to come and pour out our concerns and cares to Him. Life at work and home can be hectic, making these places less than ideal for meditative prayer, but regularly visiting Christ in the tabernacle provides a beautiful opportunity for contemplation. These visits don't even have to be long. Whenever St. Josemaría would pass a Catholic Church, he stopped if possible to take at least a few minutes in prayer before the tabernacle, conversing with the Lord in this intimate setting.

Another vital component to a life of holiness is regular Confession. Although it has been a bedrock of the spiritual life for two millennia, Sacramental Confession, unfortunately, has been the "forgotten sacrament" in many quarters of the Church in recent years. The Church requires that every Catholic go to Confession at least once a year, but St. Josemaría, aligning himself with many spiritual masters, recommended Confession on a much more frequent schedule—advising people to go weekly if possible. Through this sacrament we are, of course, forgiven our sins, including mortal sins, but it accomplishes so much more: it gives us strength to fight against those persistent venial sins that cling to us so tightly. By going to Confession frequently, we acknowledge our fallen natures and lean on the Lord as we seek to overcome our faults and weaknesses. We can never receive too much grace, so we can never go to Confession too much!

Although the Plan of Life mostly consists of daily or weekly activities, it is also of vital importance to take time on an annual basis to recharge our spiritual batteries and take stock of where we are in life. One of the primary dangers of living in the midst of the world is that we get consumed by our daily tasks without seeing the "big picture" of a life of holiness. St. Josemaría recommended that every person take an annual spiritual retreat to reflect on his progress in the spiritual life and listen to the Lord. By physically separating ourselves from our daily tasks and responsibilities on retreat, we give our minds the freedom to see beyond them and more deeply into the mysteries of God in our lives.

With the guideposts provided to us by the Plan of Life, we aim to make each moment an offering to God for His glory.

> It is vitally necessary that we be souls of prayer at all times, at every opportunity and in the most varied of circumstances, because God never abandons us. It is not a proper Christian attitude to look upon friendship with God only as a last resort. Do we think it normal to ignore or neglect the people we love? Obviously not! Those we love figure constantly in our conversations, desires and thoughts. We hold them ever present. So it should be with God.[58]

---

[58] Escrivá, *Friends of God*, 247.

We hold God "ever present." That means that there is no division of time between work and prayer—no, we must have what St. Josemaría called "unity of life." As contemplatives in the midst of the world, we offer to God as one sacrifice of praise both the times we set aside for prayer and the work we make a prayer. Let us learn next how it is we sanctify the time we spend in work.

READ

Read the chapter "Interior Life" in *Furrow* (available free online at https://www.escrivaworks.org).

MEDITATE

Meditate on the following:

"Personal sanctity is a remedy for everything!"[59]

- Do I see personal sanctity as my most important goal?
- Does my daily life reflect a plan to grow in holiness?

PRAY

- Pray for the grace to want to pray.
- Ask for opportunities to help others strengthen their interior life.

CONTEMPLATE

Visit the Blessed Sacrament and contemplate the goodness of God.

[59] Escrivá, *Furrow,* 653.

Chapter 7

Make Your Work a Way to Heaven

"Four score and seven years ago ..." "We the people ..." "When in the course of human events ..." Americans instantly recognize these phrases because they are the opening words of some of the greatest works in U.S. history: the Gettysburg Address, the Constitution, and the Declaration of Independence. The first words of an important historical document come to represent the whole document, so most writers are aware that the opening phrase must be carefully written, for it may have an impact far greater than the few words' true meaning.

With that in mind, note the first words ever said by God to the human race. In Genesis 1:28–30, we read, "Be fruitful and multiply, and fill the earth and subdue it; and have dominion over the fish of the sea and over the birds of the air and over every living thing that moves upon the earth."

The first thing God said to His people was a command to work: they were to be fruitful, conquer the earth, and be masters of all living things. And this command came before the Fall, so work is not a consequence of sin.

However, sin did have a profound effect on work, as we see after the Fall when God tells Adam,

> Because you have listened to the voice of your wife, and have eaten of the tree of which I commanded you, 'You shall not eat of it,' cursed is the ground because of you; in toil you shall eat of it all the days of your life; thorns and thistles it shall bring forth to you; and you shall eat the plants of the field. In the sweat of your face you shall eat bread till you return to the ground, for out of it you were taken; you are dust, and to dust you shall return. (Gen. 3:17–19)

Whereas before man was in harmony with nature and all living things, now he would have toil and trouble in his work. But even the Fall did not completely obliterate the dignity of work; just as sin deforms but does not destroy the goodness of man, so, too, work remains inherently something good, because its source is God. Work, in fact, still fulfills the original command of God that we subdue the earth, and our work is therefore our means of serving God.

But work is not simply an obligation that each person must fulfill in obedience to some ancient divine command. Work is also the primary battlefield in our quest for holiness. In essence, holiness is following the will of God in each moment of life, and the majority of our waking hours is spent on work in some form or another. If one can only grow in holiness through "sacred" activities—going to Mass, volunteering at the parish, or spiritual reading—then how can the young professional whose work week includes sixty hours at the office and another ten commuting ever hope to achieve the goal of every human life, which is sanctity? How can the mother of three children under age five have even a minute to devote to becoming holy? By making even our "secular" activities into a means of drawing closer to Him. God, in His great mercy, enters into all our activities, not just those explicitly reserved for Him.

Note that "work" is not limited to our paying jobs — work also encompasses our responsibilities at home, our relationships, and all we do for others. "Work," in other words, is everything we "do." We must sanctify our ordinary life, and ordinary life is the world of work.

> Work is part and parcel of man's life on earth. It involves effort, weariness, exhaustion: signs of the suffering and struggle that accompany human existence and that point to the reality of sin and the need for redemption. But in itself work is not a penalty or a curse or a punishment: those who speak of it that way have not understood sacred Scripture properly.
>
> It is time for us Christians to shout from the rooftops that work is a gift from God and that it makes no sense to classify men differently, according to their occupation, as if some jobs were nobler than others. Work, all work, bears witness to the dignity of man, to his dominion over creation. It is an opportunity to develop one's personality. It is a bond of union with others, the way to support one's family, a means of aiding in the improvement of the society in which we live and in the progress of all humanity.[60]

In 1931, St. Josemaría had one of the most formative experiences of his life while he was celebrating Mass for the Feast of the Transfiguration. Years later he would write about this day:

> That day of the Transfiguration, while celebrating Holy Mass at the Foundation for the Sick (on a side altar), when I raised the host there was another voice, without the sound of speech.

[60] Escrivá, *Christ is Passing By*, 47.

A voice, perfectly clear as always, said, *Et ego, si exaltatus fuero a terra, omnia traham ad me ipsum!* ["And I, when I am lifted up from the earth, will draw all things to myself!" (John 12:32)]. "And here is what I mean by this: I am not saying it in the sense in which it is said in Scripture. I say it to you meaning that you should put me at the pinnacle of all human activities, so that in every place in the world there will be Christians with a dedication that is personal and totally free—Christians who will be other Christs."[61]

This idea—that Christ should be at the pinnacle of all human activities—became the driving force in St. Josemaría's preaching. He put a particular emphasis on the "all" of John's words that Christ will "draw all things" to Himself—Christ is not just to be glorified at Mass or in prayer, but in every one of our activities. Work, family life, and human relationships should all be directed toward Him and offered to Him.

As Christ was glorified on Mt. Tabor, so can we glorify Him through our ordinary work. As His followers, we can make our ordinary work something extraordinary: "You cannot forget that any worthy, noble, and honest work at the human level can—and should!—be raised to the supernatural level, becoming a divine task."[62]

Offer Your Work to God

As a priest, St. Josemaría daily offered the Eucharistic sacrifice on the altar for God—this was the work that he made his "first fruits." But what about all those who are not ordained priests? Do they have nothing to offer? Scripture says that every disciple of Christ

---

61 Escrivá, "Letter, Dec. 29, 1947/Feb. 14, 1966, no. 89," in *The Founder of Opus Dei: The Life of Josemaría Escrivá, Volume I*, 326.
62 Escrivá, *The Forge*, 687.

is a priest (see 1 Pet. 2:9), and so all of us must offer sacrifice to the Lord. We do this by offering our work to the Lord; thus, our desk, our workbench, our kitchen counter—these become the "altar" on which we offer our work to the Lord. Work, therefore, is not an obstacle to holiness; rather, it is the means by which holiness is achieved.

Making our work a holy offering to God can be a struggle, however. Many of the faithful work in a secular environment that may be hostile to religion in general and Catholicism in particular. It is not uncommon for professional work environments to be filled with foul language, racy discussions, and other activities inimical to the Catholic Faith. And the home is no sanctuary: the modern media has been nothing if not relentless in finding ways to pipe such content into our homes through TV, radio, and the Internet. It might make us tempted to think that holiness can only be achieved by flight from the world. But God does not call the majority of His children to separate themselves from such a world; instead, He calls us to be salt and light in it.

Maintaining proper priorities will help us offer our work to God and grow in holiness through it. Most practicing Catholics would agree that the order of our priorities should be God, family, and work. But over time we can allow this order to become inverted without even noticing it—the ten minutes extra we stay at work as an exception quickly becomes one to two additional hours each day. We eventually even adapt our schedule to the "extra" time instead of working as efficiently as possible to get home to our family. Or we can tell a slight mistruth (telling ourselves "it won't hurt anyone") when marketing our company's product, hoping that it will help us meet the quarterly sales quota. Slowly—and subtly—we put our work ahead of faithfulness to God and to our families.

Similar dangers exist in the family. How many of us started thinking about our child's college education before we even left the maternity ward? We seem to hope they will absorb their Catholic Faith by osmosis rather than by living and learning it day in and day out through the efforts of their parents. On the other hand, we break our backs helping them achieve the highest levels of secular education. If the goal of every person is to be with God in Heaven for eternity, shouldn't we spend at least as much energy on their spiritual formation? In similar fashion, we urge our older children to delay marriage and parenthood long enough to be financially "established." But by doing so, we implicitly support a culture that looks upon children as a burden, or something extraneous to a fulfilling life.

I know a wonderful couple with eight children who, when they got engaged in their early 20s, were in a situation in which many parents advise their children to delay marriage—for the simple reason that they did not have a high-paying job and a home already lined up. But they knew that such concerns, while well-meaning, overemphasized financial "security" to the neglect of other important considerations. They chose to live frugally and trust in the Lord, and now they preside over a happy, loving, large family that witnesses the Gospel of Life to countless neighbors and friends.

Make the Secular Sacred

Even those who are serious about their faith can end up living a "double life" —on the one hand they have their secular activities—work, recreation, and family life—and on the other hand they have their "sacred" life—church, prayer, and charitable work. They believe that it is in their "sacred" lives that they are closer to God, and in their secular lives they just try to avoid falling into serious sin. But this is not integrated Christian living; it is not a complete offering to God.

God is calling you to serve Him in and from the ordinary, material, and secular activities of human life. He waits for us every day, in the laboratory, in the operating theatre, in the army barracks, in the university chair, in the factory, in the workshop, in the fields, in the home, and in all the immense panorama of work. Understand this well: there is something holy, something divine, hidden in the most ordinary situations, and it is up to each one of you to discover it.

I often said to the university students and workers who were with me in the thirties that they had to know how to 'materialize' their spiritual life. I wanted to keep them from the temptation, so common then and now, of living a kind of double life. On one side, an interior life, a life of relation with God; and on the other, a separate and distinct professional, social, and family life, full of small earthly realities.

No! We cannot lead a double life. We cannot be like schizophrenics, if we want to be Christians. There is just one life, made of flesh and spirit. And it is this life which has to become, in both soul and body, holy and filled with God. We discover the invisible God in the most visible and material things.[63]

Holiness is not something we try to snatch during short bursts of sacred activities—a Rosary here, a Mass or Examination of Conscience there. Instead, every activity of life holds out to us an invitation to grow in sanctity. Doing an excellent job on a work project or taking time out to read a book to your child, especially when

[63] Escrivá, *Conversations with Josemaria Escriva*, 114.

these acts are consciously chosen out of love for God—these things are part of following the will of God in our lives, and therefore deepen our relationship with Him.

All of our activities, if offered to Christ, can lead us closer to God. As we sanctify our work, our work sanctifies us. But this is wholly dependent upon our attitude toward our work. If we look at washing the dishes as a duty that simply must be accomplished, then it quickly becomes something that distracts us from serving God. But if we see washing those dishes as a holy act—one that glorifies God because it is His will for us at this moment, then that job is elevated from a mere earthly activity to a heavenly one.

The dichotomy that pits "secular" work against prayer, therefore, is a false one; our work is not opposed to prayer—our work, when united to Christ's redemptive work, becomes our prayer.

> Work is born of love; it is a manifestation of love and is directed toward love. We see the hand of God, not only in the wonders of nature, but also in our experience of work and effort. Work thus becomes prayer and thanksgiving, because we know we are placed on earth by God, that we are loved by Him and made heirs to His promises. We have been rightly told, "In eating, in drinking, in all that you do, do everything for God's glory."[64]

As Christians, we can also offer up our work in union with our Lord for our intentions. St. Paul mysteriously wrote, "I rejoice in my sufferings for your sake, and in my flesh I complete what is lacking in Christ's afflictions for the sake of his body, that is, the church" (Col. 1:24). In some way, Paul's sufferings are united to Christ's sufferings and are used for the benefit of the Church.

---

[64] Escrivá, *Christ Is Passing By*, 48.

Likewise, all of our work—washing dishes, building houses, correcting homework—can be united to Christ's redemptive work for the benefit of others. That project at work you are dreading can be offered for the salvation of your anti-Catholic co-worker. Need to clean the oven? Offer it for the son who is leading a profligate lifestyle. The report that is due tomorrow can be offered to strengthen a failing marriage. God takes all of the work we offer to Him—imperfect as it may be—and uses it in some mysterious way for the good of others. Work is not just something that we must do before we can enjoy ourselves, it is a powerful means to our salvation and the salvation of others.

Take Flight from Fantasy

We will find it no easy task to achieve holiness through our work, afflicted as it is with two effects of the Fall. First, our weakened natures struggle to carry out our responsibilities—we are lazy and seek pleasure and comfort. To make matters worse, we live surrounded by other fallen creatures, who seek their own pleasure and comfort. So no matter where we turn, hard work is shunned and avoided! Furthermore, we are under relentless pressure to compromise our faith—to accept the lies of this world and the prince of this world—both in our work and our family life.

Because of these pressures, we may be tempted to think that if we could just change our state in life, we could avoid those struggles. In ancient days, very few people had the opportunity to change their lot in life, so few even considered it. But today, when people change jobs—and even spouses—as easily as changing their shirts, such temptations can weigh very heavily indeed. We look at our life circumstances—a disappointing career or limited resources, for example—and believe that if these circumstances would just change, then we could really serve the Lord fully. We are like Tevye from Fiddler on the Roof, who thought that if he were a rich man, then — and only then — he would have all the time in the world to pray and read spiritual books.

Like modern-day Tevyes, we whisper to ourselves, "If I could just get out of this job, I could really spend more time serving the Lord in prayer and good works," or "If I hadn't married, then I could have served the Lord completely." Although we believe that different life circumstances would lead to a holier life, a holier life depends much more upon how we respond to our circumstances, and less on the circumstances themselves.

For a number of years I went to the same priest regularly for Confession. Young and enthusiastic, Fr. Woods was always compassionate and merciful to me while I recounted my sins. With one exception. I mentioned to him once that I was struggling with the responsibilities of being a husband and father, and made a comment that a life of holiness would be easier if I were single or a priest. Although I considered it an offhand remark, Fr. Woods immediately — and surprisingly — admonished me. He recognized my comment as a dangerous thought even to entertain, for he knew that such an attitude could grow and end up destroying my soul. He stressed to me that every vocation and state in life has its challenges, and it is spiritual suicide to fantasize that some other vocation — any vocation other than my own — would lead to a better, holier life. Although I was initially taken aback by his strong words, I came to realize the wisdom — and love — behind them.

Sanctify your everyday lives. And with these words I refer to the whole programme of your task as Christians. Stop dreaming. Leave behind false idealisms, fantasies, and what I usually call mystical wishful thinking: If only I hadn't married; if only I had a different job or qualification; if only I were in better health; if only I were younger; if only I were older. Instead, turn to the most material and immediate reality, which is where our Lord is: Look at my hands and my feet, said the risen Jesus, be assured that it is myself; touch me and see; a spirit has not flesh and bones, as you see that I have.[65]

No matter where we are in life we are going to meet challenges. Almost every job has co-workers who are annoying or even offensive. And I do mean every job—ask some mothers of potty-training toddlers how pleasant their "co-workers" are! Likewise, almost every job has responsibilities that are monotonous or exhausting. In these situations there are two possible responses: fight or flee. Will you fight to serve the Lord through these challenges, or will you flee to supposedly greener pastures? The saint faces these challenges and offers them to God for His glory; by befriending the difficult co-worker and embracing the demanding tasks, He unites these difficulties to the Cross and makes them part of our redemption.

No honorable job and no state in life is in itself an obstacle to holiness. St. Paul wrote, "Every one should remain in the state in which he was called" (1 Cor. 7:20). Desiring to alter our present situation simply because we feel that we can pursue holiness better in some other circumstance makes holiness a "dis-incarnate" reality. The tendency toward dis-incarnation—Gnosticism, or the belief that the spiritual world is unrelated to physical reality—has sprung up in many forms throughout the Church's history. However, the Incarnation of our Lord, as the Church has always insisted, proves the importance of the physical world and our everyday lives. Today's

[65] Josemaría Escrivá, *In Love with the Church* (New York: Scepter Publishing, 1989), 54. Accessed at https://www.escrivaworks.org/book/in_love_with_the_church.htm.

form of Gnosticism believes that holiness can only be pursued in some "perfect" (and future) life circumstance. We dream of a fantasy world that would supposedly lead us closer to God, all the while ignoring the possibility of growing in sanctity in our current life state. Holiness becomes a fantastical pursuit that will never be satisfied in the real world.

> How anxious people are to get out of place! Think what would happen if each bone and each muscle of the human body wanted to occupy some position other than that proper to it.
>
> There is no other reason for the world's discontent. Persevere in your place, my son; there ... what work you can do to establish our Lord's true kingdom![66]

We all seem to struggle with restlessness—when we are in college, we are anxious to graduate; when we are engaged, we want to be married; when we get our first job, we dream of the next, better one. Some of this restlessness comes from our heart's recognition that we are made for more than this world. But we must recognize that God places us in this world in a particular time, place, and circumstance that we might grow more and more into His likeness. Holiness is not dependent upon a specific outward state of affairs; no matter where we are in life, we can use our circumstances as a means for our sanctification.

Work Out Your Salvation

The past few decades have seen many technological advances in how we work, and although they promise to simplify our lives, most of these advances simply stretch the work week into a 24/7

[66] Escrivá, *The Way,* 832.

activity. Embedded in modern life is the potential for our work to overwhelm us and control our lives; no matter the time of day or where we are, our boss has instant access to us. When a client needs something, he is able to reach us even if we are on vacation with our family. In such a culture we need practical means to remind ourselves throughout each day why we work and who we ultimately work for.

So how can altars pleasing to the Lord be erected in our workplaces? If we are creative, we can find many ways to keep our hearts in tune with God as we work. A family cook St. Josemaría admired would calculate the time it took to hard boil an egg by reciting the creed twice.[67] By this simple exercise, she directed her ordinary work to God. St. Josemaría recommended that during our work we frequently glance at a crucifix or make short aspirations — "Jesus, I love you!" In these small ways, we do not allow our work to control us and overwhelm us, but instead are reminded to offer our work to God. A friend tells me that she often says in her heart, "Thank you, Jesus!" as she cares for her young children. It never fails, she says, to open her eyes anew to the amazing gift her children are. Thus, by love is she inspired to make the prayer, and the prayer, in turn, inspires love.

The daily sufferings that are part of our work offer occasions for these loving aspirations, too. Humiliated in front of colleagues, snapped at by our spouse, or ignored at a party, we can make the simple prayer, "Thank you, Jesus." How often saying this — not because we are feeling grateful, but as an act of will when we feel pride rising in our heart — results in an actual feeling of gratitude!

---

[67] William Keenan, *The Day the Bells Rang Out: St. Josemaría Escrivá and the Origins of Opus Dei* (Herefordshire: Gracewing Publishing, 2004), 13.

Pope John Paul II once got his hand slammed and trapped in a locked car door. As his driver fumbled frantically to open the door, the pope was heard to murmur, "Thank you, Jesus." In the classic book *The Way of the Pilgrim*, a wandering Russian peasant struggles to follow Paul's command to "pray without ceasing" (1 Thess. 5:17). He finally finds his solace in continually repeating the "Jesus Prayer," that classic Eastern monastic prayer, "Lord Jesus Christ, have mercy on me, a sinner." By doing this, the peasant hopes to keep his mind and heart constantly in tune with the Lord and His will. Of course, such a practice would be difficult, if not impossible, for someone working as a computer programmer or an accountant. Yet the underlying principle of intimacy with God throughout the day is still applicable — by regularly, if not constantly, making aspirations to God, we keep our minds and hearts from drifting too far away from Him. Such aspirations forge a bond between us and God, and between our souls and our work, so that everything we do can be offered to Him.

But our interaction with the Lord can consist of more than mental thoughts and prayers; the Incarnation shows us the importance of the physical world in the plan of our salvation. Thus physical reminders of our Lord and the saints — a little crucifix on the desk, a picture of a saint above the kitchen sink — keep our mind fixed on God and our path to Him while we work. A holy priest I know always recommends to families that they have a crucifix or holy picture in every room of the house, so that no matter where they are they can always lift their eyes to God.

Also, making small gestures, such as the sign of the Cross or a kiss of a picture of our Lady, tunes us into the world of Heaven even in the midst of earthly affairs. In a culture that bombards us with images contrary to Gospel living, we can counteract such impressions with Catholic iconography, as a result keeping our hearts and minds close to the Lord throughout the workday.

For the saint, work and a life of prayer are inseparable. Although it is vital to stay committed to a plan of prayer for each day, it would be a mistake to think that these are the only times we grow in holiness. Growing in sanctity is a holistic effort that unites the times we set aside for prayer with the work we make a prayer in one complete offering to God.

St. Paul implores every Christian to "work out your own salvation with fear and trembling" (Phil. 2:12). The primary place in which we work out our salvation is work itself, and so the importance of work in the life of holiness cannot be overemphasized. Sanctity involves the transformation of the whole person, and thus the activity that consumes the majority of our lives—work—is instrumental in determining whether that transformation will take place. St. Josemaría said that work is "the hinge on which our calling to sanctity rests and turns."[68] If we do not recognize work as the battlefield in the fight for holiness, then surely we have already lost.

---

[68] Escrivá, *Friends of God*, 62.

READ

Read the chapter "Working for God" in *Friends of God* (available free online at http://www.escrivaworks.org).

MEDITATE

Meditate on the following passage from the Gospel of John:

> *"And I, when I am lifted up from the earth, will draw all men to myself." (John 12:32)*

- Do I draw all the things of my life to Christ?
- How can my work draw me and those around me to Christ?

PRAY

- Offer up your difficulties at work for a suffering friend or relative.
- Pray for those looking for a job to support their family.

CONTEMPLATE

Consider the salvific importance of the "hidden years" of Jesus.

Chapter 8

Live in the Family of God

The folk tale of the boy raised by wolves has appealed to the imaginations of children and adults for generations. What would a person be like who had no human family? How would he act? What would be his moral compass? Could he be integrated into human society as an adult? The fascination with this story is due to the fact that everyone instinctively understands the importance of family in the development of the human person. It is in the family that one learns right and wrong, how to interact with others, and the priorities of a well-lived life.

In the spiritual life, too, our formation occurs in a family—our natural family, yes, but more importantly, the family of God. At our baptisms, we become children of God, but also we enter into the family of God, the Church. Our spiritual life and development is not an isolated affair, but something that occurs within the context of the living Church. St. Josemaría had a deep devotion to the Church, recognizing it as indispensable in the life of the Christian. His attitude toward the Church can be summed up in one of his favorite phrases, "To Jesus through Mary with Peter."[69]

---

[69] Escrivá, *Christ Is Passing By*, 139.

St. Josemaría Escrivá lived in a time of great upheaval in the Church. In the 1960s, scores of priests and members of religious orders forsook their vows, and multitudes of Catholics left the Church, never to return. But again and again St. Josemaría urged people to remain loyal to the Church and be dutiful children: "In that cry *serviam*! you express your determination to 'serve' the Church of God most faithfully, even at the cost of fortune, of reputation, and of life."[70] St. Josemaría recognized that although many members of the Church may fail and even sin grievously, scandal does not provide an excuse for leaving the confines of the Church. The Church is not simply an institution; the Church, first and foremost, is a family—and would, or could, you leave your family just because your siblings sinned? Familial bonds go beyond simple agreement on life principles; they are forged in blood, or, in the case of the Church, Christ's blood. The familial aspects of the Faith are the foundation for lasting loyalty to the Church.

Faithfulness to the Church is not an "auxiliary" part of practicing the Christian Faith, but an integral part of a life devoted to sanctification. In our individualistic age, we tend to look at everything—including our sanctification and salvation—as self-contained pursuits that are carried out without relationship to others. But if we carefully consider our interdependence with others, we can see how ludicrous this is. Would a wife striving for holiness have the attitude that her husband could just fend for himself? Of course not—she understands that she is intimately bound to her spouse and their steps towards sanctity—or away from it—are taken together. The interpersonal communion we have with others is rooted in our creation in the image and likeness of God. Pope John Paul II said that the Triune God is a "family,"[71] and therefore, as images of Him,

---

[70] Escrivá, *The Way*, 519.
[71] Scott Hahn, *First Comes Love* (New York: Image Books, 2002), 42.

we are communal beings. The process of our sanctification is thus a communal activity: we are helped along the way by our brothers and sisters in the Faith, and we are obligated to help them too, as we all work toward our final goal — the communion of Father, Son, and Holy Spirit.

Love Mary

Another mark of the loyal son of God is devotion to His mother, the Blessed Virgin Mary. Looking over the writings of St. Josemaría, one might note that he never wrote an extended treatise on Mary. But this should not be taken as evidence of a lack of devotion on his part, for to St. Josemaría, Mary was like the air: her presence permeated his thoughts and was an integral part of his spirituality. In almost every writing and every homily, St. Josemaría naturally wove in his love for the Blessed Mother, begging for her intercession and identifying her as the perfect model of all virtues and a life of prayer.

Mary is an essential part of an authentically Christian life. Today many Christians, even Catholics, look upon Mary as an "extra" in the path to sanctification. St. Josemaría could not have disagreed more; he believed that devotion to our Blessed Mother leads us on a sure path to Christ. Our devotion to Mary should be based on the reality that she is our mother. As we are fellow sons of God with Jesus Christ, the Eternal Son of God, so, too, do we have Mary for our mother as He did. On the Cross, Jesus said to His beloved disciple, "Behold your mother" (John 19:27), thus making sons of Mary all His beloved disciples. And as John took Mary into his home that day, so we, too, need to take Mary into our homes, our hearts.

Nor is Mary's motherhood some dry, theological concept. We do not remain distant from our earthly mothers, keeping them at arm's length during our struggles and successes. "How does a normal son or daughter treat his mother? In different ways, of course, but always affectionately and confidently, never coldly. In an intimate way, through small, commonplace customs. And a mother feels hurt if we omit them: a kiss or an embrace when leaving or coming home, a little extra attention, a few warm words. In our relationship with our mother in Heaven, we should act in very much the same way."[72] Over the centuries countless devotions to our Lady have arisen, and this is a wonderful sign of our desire for intimacy with her. Each devotion — such as the Rosary or the scapular or kissing the feet of statues of Mary — reflects an intimate affection for the mother Christ gave to each of us. We come to her when we encounter both toils and triumphs with confidence that through them she will help us to draw closer to her son Jesus.

This affectionate attitude toward Mary helps us to become better children of God; it allows us to see ourselves more clearly as small, humble children who need help. "To become children we must renounce our pride and self-sufficiency, recognizing that we can do nothing by ourselves. We must realize that we need grace, and the help of God our Father to find our way and keep to it. To be little, you have to abandon yourself as children do, believe as children believe, beg as children beg. And we learn all this through contact with Mary."[73] One of the beautiful marks of Marian devotion is humility, because the Blessed Mother is the epitome of the humble servant. She is the greatest of all of God's creations, yet her true greatness lies in humility to God's will. She only wants what God wants — nothing more, nothing less. Humility is death to self and submission to God: Mary more than anyone exemplifies this

---

[72] Escrivá, *Christ Is Passing By,* 142.
[73] Escrivá, *Christ Is Passing By,* 143.

essential virtue. Those who are devoted to Mary can model their own lives on this humble woman.

Devotion to Mary as our mother likewise makes us better children of the Church: "Mary continually builds the Church and keeps it together. It is difficult to have devotion to our Lady and not feel closer to the other members of the mystical body and more united to its visible head, the pope."[74] Our intimate relationship with Mary unites us more deeply to all her children in the Church. When one of them is suffering, we suffer. When one of them falls, we help pick them up. And when we fall, we turn to them for help. Mary unites her children into one loving family.

Non-Catholic Christians protest that devotion to our Lady harms our devotion to the Lord. Our focus should be solely on Jesus, according to this way of thinking, not on His human mother or any other creature. But this attitude misunderstands the role of Mary, and the reason God gave her to His beloved disciples. Mary's sole purpose is to deepen our love for Christ, to send us further on the path of sanctity that ends in Jesus. As Mary said at the wedding of Cana, we are to "do whatever he tells [us]" (John 2:5) — making the will of God the utmost priority in our lives. "The beginning of the way, at the end of which you will find yourself completely carried away by love for Jesus, is a trusting love for Mary."[75]

In Mary we find the "secret" of sanctity: not great deeds or bold words, but a humble submission to the will of God in the ordinary things of life. Mary, the greatest of all God's creatures, lived her earthly life as an ordinary housewife.

We can't forget that Mary spent nearly every day of her life just like millions of other women who look after their

[74] Ibid., 139.
[75] Ibid., 143.

family, bring up their children, and take care of the house. Mary sanctifies the ordinary everyday things — what some people wrongly regard as unimportant and insignificant: everyday work, looking after those closest to you, visits to friends and relatives. What a blessed ordinariness, that can be so full of love of God!

For that's what explains Mary's life — her love. A complete love, so complete that she forgets herself and is happy just to be there where God wants her, fulfilling with care what God wants her to do. That is why even her slightest action is never routine or vain but, rather, full of meaning. Mary, our mother, is for us both an example and a way. We have to try to be like her, in the ordinary circumstances in which God wants us to live.[76]

Mary had the perfect childlike attitude toward her heavenly Father, and we should model that attitude. When the angel Gabriel told her she was to be with child by the power of the Holy Spirit, she responded simply, "let it be to me according to your word" (Luke 1:38). When a child is on a walk with her father, she does not keep track of where she is — she simply trusts that her loving father will guide her home. Mary trusted completely in the promises of God and knew that, if she followed Him faithfully, He would lead her home. We, too, must have the childlike devotion that Mary did, modeling our lives after that of this perfect disciple.

Be in Union with the Pope

St. Josemaría loved to say, "To Jesus Through Mary with Peter." It is these three individuals who sum up the essence of the Catholic

76 Ibid., 148.

life. We of course follow Jesus in all things. We come to Jesus through His Blessed Mother. And we are united to Jesus by being united to the successor of St. Peter, the Pope. As Catholics, we are called to follow Christ within the Church based in Rome and led by the pope. There exists no authority to create a Church molded to our preferences. Rather, we are invited to submit ourselves to the Church founded by Christ on the rock of Peter. Devotion to anything but this rightful authority will tend to denigrate into a self-serving individualism. St. Josemaría expressed this devotion to the Catholic Church with the title Roman: "The Catholic Church is Roman. I savour that word, Roman! I feel completely Roman, since Roman means universal, catholic. For it leads me to love tenderly the Pope, il dolce Cristo in terra, as Saint Catherine of Siena, whom I count as a most beloved friend, liked to repeat."[77] The title "Roman" paradoxically means "universal," or catholic, because Rome is the center of a Church that spread throughout the world. "All roads lead to Rome." By striving to be "Roman," Catholics are able to think with the mind of the Church and remain faithfully within God's family.

The paradox of a universal church centered in a single city has many times throughout Christian history seemed a scandal. Many opposed to the Church have tried to diminish or even reject Rome's importance in the life of the Church: How can one city be so instrumental for fulfilling God's plan of salvation? Such arguments fail to see that this is God's way of working in the world. The nation of Israel was a small, insignificant country — but God used it to change the world. Jesus was a poor carpenter in a backwater town in a forgotten district of the Roman Empire — yet He is the way to

[77] Josemaría Escrivá, *In Love With the Church*, 11.

salvation for all people. God uses specific people, nations, and cities to be the means by which He brings people to Him. Rome, by the providence of God, has been appointed the home of the unifying center of the Church, and so all Christians need to be "Roman," no matter where they live.

Of course, Rome is the center of the Church because it is the see of the successor to St. Peter, the pope. The pope is called our "Holy Father," and he is to be treated as a dutiful son would treat his father—with love and respect. "For me, in the hierarchy of love, the Pope comes right after the Most Holy Trinity and our Mother the Virgin."[78] This isn't an unthinking obeisance, like a slave to a master, but instead the filial obedience a son has to his father.

This obedience can be a challenge, especially in those times when it seems like the Holy Father isn't doing what we think is right. But we need to approach those situations as sons. Let's say a son believed his father was poorly treating his mother. What is he to do? First, he must give his father the benefit of the doubt. He makes sure he is clear about what his father is doing, taking steps to not make any mistakes in understanding. He asks his father (and his mother) questions. If after doing so the son is still uneasy, he does not do anything unless he is sure the mistreatment is happening. Only when he has significant reason, formed by a full understanding of the situation, to believe his mother is being poorly treated does he take action to challenge his father. But even in this we see a filial obedience, because taking action in this case is best for his father.

Ultimately, St. Josemaria's desire for Catholics to be "with Peter" stresses the essential importance of being in communion with the pope. In today's age of scandals and disappointments with the

---

[78] Escrivá, *Conversations with Josemaria Escriva*, 46.

Church, it might be easy to look to "greener pastures" like Eastern Orthodoxy or Protestantism. Yet we are part of a family, and children don't disown their father, even if the father isn't perfect (as no father is). They stay in the family and work for its salvation, even—especially—the salvation of the father himself. To be "with Peter" is to be a part of the Catholic Church, the family of God.

Honor St. Joseph

St. Josemaría also had a great devotion to another member of our "family:" St. Joseph. He encouraged others to do so as well. In fact, early in life he combined his first two names—José and Maria—into one to show his deep love for the earthly parents of Christ. St. Joseph was integral to St. Josemaría's spirituality, and he believed the earthly father of Jesus was both a great model and intercessor for all those pursuing holiness in the world.

As a way of affection and devotion, St. Josemaría always called Joseph by two titles: "father" and "lord":

> St Joseph really is a father and lord. He protects those who revere him and accompanies them on their journey through this life—just as he protected and accompanied Jesus when he was growing up. As you get to know him, you discover that the holy patriarch is also a master of the interior life—for he teaches us to know Jesus and share our life with Him, and to realize that we are part of God's family. St Joseph can teach us these lessons, because he is an ordinary man, a family man, a worker who earned his living by manual labour—all of which has great significance and is a source of happiness for us.[79]

[79] Escrivá, *Christ Is Passing By,* 39.

Joseph is our father because he is the father of Jesus, our brother. We should not diminish Joseph's fatherhood simply because he was not biologically related to Jesus. The Second Person of the Trinity had to submit Himself to Joseph's headship in the Holy Family, and He did so willingly. Joseph guided and protected the child Jesus, always placing his son's welfare before his own. Will he not do likewise for us when we make him our father as well?

Furthermore, Joseph is our "lord" because he can lead us in the spiritual life. This reflects St. Josemaría's favorite description of Joseph: "master of the interior life." Why? Because "interior life is nothing but continual and direct conversation with Christ, so as to become one with him,"[80] and no one, other than Mary, had more intimate contact with Jesus. Joseph's contact with Jesus took place in the same context in which most of us must approach Jesus: through work and family. Joseph spent countless hours at the carpenter's bench, working with Jesus on his latest projects. He was able to combine a diligent work ethic with a deep intimacy with Jesus. And this is the path to holiness for each of us: living our ordinary lives in close and constant contact with the Lord.

Joseph then becomes the teacher of an interior life lived in the midst of the world. "Who could be a better teacher for us than St. Joseph? If you want my advice, which I have never tired of repeating these many years, *Ite ad Ioseph*: 'Go to Joseph.' He will show us definite ways, both human and divine, to approach Jesus."[81] Joseph was an ordinary man caught up in an extraordinary situation and called to extraordinary works. Yet he responded with tranquility and obedience. When he found his fiancé with child, he did not become distraught or depressed; he thought first of her honor and

80 Ibid., 56.
81 Ibid., 38.

desired to protect her name. When danger threatened his family from the highest levels of power, he took Mary and Jesus to a foreign country in obedience to God's messenger. And Joseph did all this with supreme humility. He is called the "silent saint," for not one word of his is recorded in the Bible. His whole life revolved around Jesus and Mary, and he did nothing to promote his own desires or wishes. No wonder St. Josemaría considered him the perfect model for those desiring to be contemplatives in the midst of the world.

St. Josemaría liked to call the Holy Family of Jesus, Mary, and Joseph the "earthly trinity" who leads us to the heavenly Trinity. Each member is essential to a deeply rooted Catholic spirituality: "Saint Joseph: One cannot love Jesus and Mary without loving the Holy Patriarch."[82] An integral part of the path to holiness is recognizing that we are members of a family; devotion to Mary and Joseph as our parents deepens that reality. We can be sure that they will always lead us to their son.

Although we are called to live in the family of God—the Church—we also live in the midst of a fallen, broken world. Are we to ignore it and do nothing to bring it closer to God? If there is one thing in common among the saints, it is that they were passionate about leading others to Christ. If we desire to be saints as well, we, too, must proclaim Christ to the world. To this concern we will look next.

---

[82] Escrivá, *The Forge*, 551.

READ

Read the chapter "Loyalty to the Church" from *In Love with the Church* (available free online at https://www.escrivaworks.org).

MEDITATE

Meditate on the following:

"What joy to be able to say with all the fervour of my soul: I love my Mother the holy Church!"[83]

- How do I love my mother, the Church, in practical deeds?
- Do I consider the Church an extraneous part of my faith, or essential to it?

PRAY

- Pray for the pope and all bishops that they may be faithful to the Lord.
- Pray daily for your parish priest(s).

CONTEMPLATE

Consider the mystical union we have with all the members of Christ's Body united through the Eucharist.

[83] Escrivá, *The Way*, 518.

Chapter 9

Proclaim Christ to the World

One of the great phenomena in the history of sociology is the incredible growth of the early Christian Church. Springing up from a small band of fishermen and other laborers in a remote section of the civilized world, the Catholic Faith in a few centuries became the dominant religion of the Roman Empire. The initial growth of the Church was powered by missionaries such as St. Paul, who took the Good News to the farthest reaches of the Empire, but after that initial burst, the Church expanded more organically, from family to family, friend to friend, and co-worker to co-worker. Once the leaven was introduced to the life of the Empire, it spread throughout Rome's lands until the Faith could be found in every corner of the Empire's boundaries.

Interestingly, early Christians were difficult to distinguish from their fellow citizens by outward appearances. They worked the same jobs, paid their taxes, and spoke the same languages as the pagans. An early Christian described their lifestyle:

> Christians are indistinguishable from other men either by nationality, language or customs. They do not inhabit separate cities of their own, or speak a strange dialect, or follow some outlandish way of life. Their teaching is not based

upon reveries inspired by the curiosity of men. Unlike some other people, they champion no purely human doctrine. With regard to dress, food, and manner of life in general, they follow the customs of whatever city they happen to be living in, whether it is Greek or foreign.[84]

In other words, the early Christians naturally blended into society in all things that did not conflict with their beliefs. But, of course, that did not make them identical to the rest of society; as Christ commanded, they were in the world, but not of it (cf. John 17:11–16). As this early Christian also notes,

And yet there is something extraordinary about their lives. They live in their own countries as though they were only passing through. They play their full role as citizens, but labor under all the disabilities of aliens. Any country can be their homeland, but for them their homeland, wherever it may be, is a foreign country. Like others, they marry and have children, but they do not expose them. They share their meals, but not their wives.[85]

The early Christians, as much as possible, lived as good Roman citizens, yet they refused to compromise their faith in order to "fit in" to the greater society.

In many ways, the challenges of the first Christians are the same as ours today. Like them, we are called to live within the world like our non-Christian neighbors—work the same jobs, buy the same clothes, eat the same food—yet we must reject the culture

---

[84] "From a Letter to Diognetus," The Holy See, accessed July 1, 2022, https://www.vatican.va/spirit/documents/spirit_20010522_diogneto_en.html.

[85] Ibid.

of death that surrounds us. We must live in society, but as though we are "only passing through," for our true home is not here but in the next world.

So how did these non-descript first Christians end up converting an entire empire? Although we most often think of the missionaries and the martyrs when we think of the spread of the early Church, most evangelization was done quietly in the homes and marketplaces of each town and city. There was no distinction within the Church between those who preached the Gospel and those who didn't: every Christian recognized it as his duty to spread the Faith in his own circle of influence, no matter how large or small. Even slaves, who were the lowest class of society and were held in contempt by the upper echelons of the culture, spread their faith by their attitude toward their masters, their treatment of their fellow slaves, and how they went about their daily tasks. Each and every Christian knew that it was his obligation to witness to the power of Christ in his life.

St. Josemaría saw this early Church model of apostolate as one that we should readopt in modern times. Having come to know the saint in these pages, it should not surprise the reader that he did not go in for a two-tiered system of evangelization, where "missionaries" spread the Faith and the rest of us only pray for their success. St. Josemaría believed that every Christian has an obligation to share the Good News of Jesus Christ — right where they are. One does not need to leave his job or home in order to evangelize; opportunities to be a witness for Christ always present themselves in the day-to-day activities of ordinary life.

Be a Faithful Friend

Today many Christians picture evangelization as going to a foreign country or door-to-door and asking strangers if they want to become Christians. As valuable as those efforts are, they were not the primary means by which the Faith spread in the early Church. Instead, Christianity expanded by what St. Josemaría called an "apostolate of friendship":

> Those well-timed words, whispered into the ear of your wavering friend; the helpful conversation that you managed to start at the right moment; the ready professional advice that improves his university work; the discreet indiscretion by which you open up unexpected horizons for his zeal. This all forms part of the "apostolate of friendship."[86]

Friendship has a powerful impact on people's behavior. Parents often worry that their children will succumb to "peer pressure," implicitly acknowledging the power that friends can have on someone's life. Children aren't the only ones influenced in this way—adults, too, allow their personalities and choices to be shaped by the company they keep. Communal-ness is part of human nature. We want to be accepted by others. We don't want to seem odd. Natural as this is, it, too, often leads people away from the Faith and into the culture of death in which we live. But friendship's power can work both ways: the Christian who remains faithful to his beliefs and stands up for Christ in this life can have a great influence over those closest to him, even without saying a word.

Loyalty and trustworthiness then are the calling of every Christian: encouraging others, helping them in need, and urging them to do the right thing. A trusted friend will be the one who is depended upon and asked for advice when the troubles of life weigh someone down. A Christian friend can be there with wise advice for the person considering a divorce or other important life decision; he can offer support for someone trying to resist the immoral culture we all live

---

[86] Escrivá, *The Way*, 973.

in. Being a true friend can be powerfully evangelistic, for everyone is more likely to listen to a friend than a stranger. This does not mean, of course, that we are friends with others just to evangelize. No, it is because we love our friends that we share our faith with them.

A key component of the apostolate of friendship is something that St. Josemaría liked to call "prestige." When this word is misinterpreted it means fame or glory. Prestige in that sense is a selfish attempt to be noticed and held in reverence or awe. This is not what St. Josemaría meant by "prestige." Instead, he intended something closer to "a good reputation." The person who is loyal, hardworking, and willing to help others—that is the person who is quietly admired by friends and acquaintances. That is the person who will be looked to as a model worth emulating. By legitimately building your prestige, you come to be a positive and Christian influence on others.

In my first job after college as a computer programmer, I tried to work in an honest and upright fashion. During my two years at this job I became friends with one of my co-workers, who was a good-natured, if foul-mouthed, agnostic. He and I never discussed my religious beliefs, although he knew I was a practicing Catholic. At the end of my last day on the job, he came into my office and closed the door. He then initiated what became a two-hour conversation about God, human nature, and the teachings of the Catholic Church. My mostly silent witness over the previous two years led him to reach out to me as he struggled to answer some of life's greatest questions. By working hard and honestly, I became someone my co-worker could seek help from on matters beyond the realm of software development. If I had been lazy, deceptive, or otherwise a poor worker, it is unlikely that we would have had that conversation.

One of the key components to building prestige is the practice of human virtues such as fortitude, composure, and patience. Catholic theology has always emphasized that grace builds upon nature: God works with our natural strengths in order to make us more like Him. This is true in the virtues as well. Human virtues are the "foundation of the supernatural ones,"[87] and it is through the practice of the human virtues that we can grow in the supernatural virtues of faith, hope, and love. Most human virtues are universally recognized as laudable, and people gravitate toward those who practice them. It is not uncommon to find in many workplaces an employee who does the bare minimum and allows others to carry his load. No one will desire to follow or emulate such a person. But the conscientious worker, who strives for excellence in his tasks, has patience when problems arise, and is compassionate to others when they are struggling — this is the person whom others will look to when they need advice or help.

Practicing the virtues well is thus an example for all to see and emulate. But one should not think that a Christian should practice the virtues only in order to be seen. "Your virtue [must] not be noisy,"[88] in other words, we must practice the virtues quietly and in humility, trusting that God will use our faithfulness to the virtues to bring others to Him. By living the virtues well — which means working hard, caring for our family, and doing well the "little things" that make up our daily lives — we become examples for others, and they will desire to know the source of our strength.

This does not mean that we have to be perfect to be a good witness. We all struggle and we all fail to live a virtuous life. But almost as important as practicing the virtues is how we react when we inevitably fall. Are we defensive? Do we blame others? Do we justify our actions? One of the primary beliefs of our Catholic Faith is that we are part of a fallen race. If we can't admit that we, too,

---

[87] Escrivá, *Friends of God*, 91.
[88] Escrivá, *The Way*, 140.

sometimes fail, then we are denying this truth. The most powerful witness is the one who always strives to live virtuously but quickly gets back up, asks forgiveness, and moves on when failing to do so.

Oftentimes, in our legitimate desire to be a good witness to others, we try to come off as perfect. A mom who pretends her children are flawless and her family life has no problems will not be a model for the struggling mom who has her hands full just keeping her kids from pulling each other's hair out. For one thing, the struggling mom will be too intimidated by Mrs. Perfect to confide in her. But the mother who admits she doesn't always do the right thing—and asks for forgiveness quickly when she falls—this is the model others can follow.

Be an Apostle, Not an Activist

What is the source of a strong life of virtue? A strong interior life. As St. Josemaría remarked, "Many years ago, as I reflected upon our Lord's way of doing things, I came to the conclusion that the apostolate, of whatever kind it be, must be an overflow of the interior life."[89] The interior life is the fuel that drives apostolate: not only does it give one the strength to persevere in the face of hardship, it gives one the desire to share his faith with others. The danger to the person who does not value the interior life is that he becomes completely self-consumed. The day consists of self-focused thoughts: What should I do today? What should I eat? What should I wear? How should I entertain myself? Instead of being directed outward, such people think only of their own needs. But the person who has a deep interior life of prayer—who spends at least some time each day in prayer with our Lord—is thus working to be directed outward. Such a person comes to desire with all his heart the good of others, which is ultimately their sanctification and salvation.

[89] Escrivá, *Friends of God*, 239.

Furthermore, an apostolate that is not grounded in a solid prayer life is doomed to devolve into simple activism: "I really do believe that a serious danger of losing the way threatens those who launch out into action—activism!—while neglecting prayer, self denial, and those means without which it is impossible to achieve a solid piety: receiving the Sacraments frequently, meditation, examination of conscience, spiritual reading, and constant recourse to Our Lady and the Guardian Angels."[90]

The danger of apostolate denigrating into simple activism is a real one. We can overload ourselves with so many "good" activities that we have no time to be quiet with the Lord. But an apostolate that does not derive from a deep interior life descends into chaos. St. Catherine of Siena was called to a deep interior prayer life at a young age. She spent many of her early years locked in her room in prayerful conversation with God. She didn't interact with anyone other than her family and her confessor, living a more cloistered life than most nuns. But then God called her to leave her room and go out into the world to work for Him. Her time of seclusion was a preparation for her great work in the world, a work that would influence nations and even the papacy. In following this call of God, however, she never stopped praying; she continued to spend hours in union with God each day.

It is the Christian's intimacy with Christ that imbues his work with meaning. Such intimacy, we know, is fostered only by a serious, sacramental life of prayer. Any work we perform in the world, whether it is for social justice or service to the poor or anything else, must be founded on prayer. While an activist is pulled from

[90] Escrivá, *Friends of God*, 18.

prayer by a desire to "get things done," the Christian knows that it is only through prayer that he can effectively do the work of God. Mother Teresa prayed fifteen decades of the Rosary each morning and spent hours on end in prayer. When a reporter once asked how, with all she had to do, she could spend so much time praying, she responded, "How can I not?"

Prayer unleashes the power of God in this world and is thus infinitely more effective than any other action we can take. St. Thérèse of Lisieux was named the patron saint of the missions even though she never stepped foot in the mission fields herself. She holds this title because of her earnest prayers for missionaries, which were more powerful and effective than any mission trip she could have taken. One who is engaged in apostolate is rooted in prayer and covets the prayers of the faithful, for he knows that any other foundation is sinking sand.

The life of the activist can be overwhelming; many setbacks and failures impede his efforts to change the world. Victories are few. Eventually, discouragement sets in and the activist is tempted to abandon the cause. But the Christian engaged in apostolate does not take stock of his efforts based on worldly success or failure. He cares only about faithfulness to God's commands. He knows that as long as he does the will of God, success or failure of a certain project is irrelevant. And worldly failure does not always mean failure in the eyes of God. The Christian's ultimate example of "failure" is the Crucifixion. Jesus was faithful to His Father's will, but in the eyes of the world, His "project" was an abject failure. And how many of His own followers thought so as well! But God's ways turn our "failures" into His successes. That is why the person involved in apostolate does not get either excited or downcast when worldly success or failure comes, for he knows that the only "success" worth striving for is faithfulness to God's Word. Mother

Teresa, who did more to help the poor in the twentieth century than any other individual, stated, "We are called upon not to be successful, but to be faithful." If she had not had that attitude, surely she would have given up early in her work, which faced countless setbacks and obstacles through the years.

The activist focused exclusively on this world asks: How can laws be made more just, how can the poor be better fed, or how can this candidate or party be made victorious? But the Christian engaged in apostolate keeps his eyes fixed on the next world. This does not mean that he is indifferent to this-world results; instead, he sees earthly goals in light of our final destination, which is Heaven. An activist might applaud a law that makes it easier to feed the poor, although it puts restrictions on the preaching of the Gospel. But the person involved in apostolate would know that there is a hierarchy of goods, and the Gospel and its proclamation always come first. As Christ said, "seek first the kingdom and his righteousness, and all these things will be given to you as well" (Matt. 6:33). Justice and peace among peoples are admirable ideals, and all Christians desire these things, but they also realize that such ideals are not our primary goals. They are the secondary results of a society that places God's kingdom first.

St. Thérèse of Lisieux compared herself to a child's ball and said she would be completely content if God desired to sit her in the corner most of the time. She only wanted to be used as He desired. We, too, should recognize our place in accomplishing God's will here on earth, instead of trying to create a place for ourselves.

Be Transformed

The goal of the Christian is not to change the world, it is to transform individuals. St. Josemaría lived in one of the most difficult centuries of humankind: he experienced the Spanish civil war firsthand, witnessed the rise of Nazi Germany and the dominance of Soviet Russia, and late in his life saw the breakdown of morality in the West. Yet throughout these crises, he emphasized that the individual heart is central: "A secret, an open secret: these world crises are crises of saints." The way to transform the culture is to transform individuals, and the way to transform individuals is to first be transformed. The best way to evangelize and transform the world is to be a saint.

A tremendous example of someone living his faith heroically in the midst of an evil world was St. Maximilian Kolbe. In spite of being surrounded by the horrendous evil of Nazism, Kolbe quietly and steadfastly refused to compromise his love for the Lord and our Lady. He continued to preach and evangelize, and eventually his work led to his arrest and imprisonment in a concentration camp. But he was yet to bear his greatest witness, while living in a truly satanic environment. For when the guards decided to kill ten men in retaliation for an escape, Kolbe offered himself in place of another prisoner who was a husband and a father. This is the essence of all apostolate: to give of yourself totally and completely for the good of others. It does not mean running from this world, but embracing it with the love of Jesus Christ.

The most famous sermon given by St. Josemaría was called, provocatively, "Passionately Loving the World." Many Christians then—and today—believed that the world was something evil to be shunned. But St. Josemaría rejected that idea: "This I have been teaching all the time, using words from holy Scripture: the world is not evil, because it comes from the hands of God, because it is His creation, because Yahweh looked upon it and saw that it was good. It is we ourselves, men and women, who make it evil and ugly with our sins and unfaithfulness."[91] It is only by being part of

---

[91] Escrivá, *In Love with the Church*, 52.

the world that we can hope to help redeem it. Christ calls each of His followers to follow Him in and through the world:

> When people [have tried to present the Christian way of life as something exclusively spiritual], churches become the setting par excellence of the Christian way of life. And being a Christian means going to church, taking part in sacred ceremonies, getting into an ecclesiastical mentality, in a special kind of world, considered the ante-chamber to heaven, while the ordinary world follows its own separate course. In this case, Christian teaching and the life of grace would pass by, brushing very lightly against the turbulent advance of human history but never coming into proper contact with it ... we flatly reject this deformed vision of Christianity.[92]

The early Christians transformed the pagan Roman Empire not by separating themselves from it, but by being good Christians — and good citizens — within it. By doing so, they became leaven that penetrated every corner of society. In today's post-Christian world, disciples of Christ are called to do the same thing — passionately love the world and transform it from within.

[92] Ibid., 51.

READ

Read the chapter "Passionately Loving the World" from In Love with the Church (available free online at https://www.escrivaworks.org).

MEDITATE

Meditate on the following:

> *"You have got to be a 'man of God,'*
> *a man of interior life, a man of prayer*
> *and sacrifice. Your apostolate must*
> *be the overflow of your life 'within.'"*[93]

- Does my interior life "overflow" to others?
- Do I pray and work for the salvation of those around me?

PRAY

- Pray for the salvation of your loved ones.
- Pray for missionaries throughout the world.

CONTEMPLATE

Consider the pouring forth of God the Father's love toward His Son as a model for apostolate.

[93] Escrivá, *The Way*, 961.

Conclusion

"This is God's will for you, your sanctification"

The twentieth century is on record as the bloodiest in human history. From the concentration camps in Nazi Germany to the gulags in Soviet Russia to the abortion clinics in America, more innocent blood was shed in the previous century than all other centuries combined. It might be legitimate to ask, "Where is God in all of this?" I think a saying of St. Josemaría, who lived through most of these terrible times, answers this question: "These world crises are crises of saints."[94] The "solution" that God gives to the world for its chosen path of death and destruction is to raise up saints who will show the world a better way to live. In the twentieth century, God led the Church to reemphasize its traditional teaching that all people are called to sainthood. The only way to overcome the world and to save it is for each and every person to live a saintly life within the world.

St. Josemaría accepted a mission from God to spread the message of the universal call to holiness and preached it tirelessly. The fact that many Catholics today take for granted this universal call — they no longer relegate holiness to a pursuit of priests and religious — is thanks in large part to the work of St. Josemaría. When many elements in the Church still insisted that the only path to true holiness

[94] Escrivá, *The Way*, 301.

was through the religious life, the Spanish saint steadfastly reiterated the message of Christ and the early Church: God wants us all to "be perfect" as he is perfect.

> We are deeply moved, and our hearts profoundly shaken, when we listen attentively to that cry of St Paul: 'This is God's will for you, your sanctification.' Today, once again, I set myself this goal and I also remind you and all mankind: this is God's Will for us, that we be saints. In order to bring peace, genuine peace, to souls; in order to transform the earth and to seek God Our Lord in the world and through the things of the world, personal sanctity is indispensable. In my conversations with people from so many countries and from all kinds of social backgrounds, I am often asked: 'What do you say to us married folk? To those of us who work on the land? To widows? To young people?'
>
> I reply systematically that I have only 'one stewing pot.' I usually go on to point out that Our Lord Jesus Christ preached the good news to all, without distinction. One stewing pot and only one kind of food: 'My food is to do the will of him who sent me, and to accomplish his work.' He calls each and every one to holiness; he asks each and every one to love him: young and old, single and married, healthy and sick, learned and unlearned, no matter where they work, or where they are.[95]

Such a lofty goal is not achieved by accident or through a halfhearted effort. It takes desire and determination to allow God's grace to work in our lives, slowly transforming us into the likeness of His Son, Jesus Christ. But the genius of St. Josemaría's teachings is that

---

[95] Escrivá, *Friends of God*, 294.

such a noble task can be obtained through both a fundamental understanding of who we are in God's eyes—beloved children—and practical steps that lead us closer to God each day. We just need to decide today that we want holiness more than anything, and that we will do anything to obtain it. Holiness need not be intimidating—it can be achieved by everyone!

Acknowledgments

In my last book, I thanked my wife Suzan last, figuring I was saving the best for last. Now I want to thank her first and foremost, for without her this book (and the last) would not have been possible. She is not only a great wife and mother, but an incredible editor. And more importantly, she is a model to me of striving for holiness in ordinary life.

I also want to thank Dr. Scott Hahn, who first introduced me to the spirituality of St. Josemaría Escrivá and who graciously agreed to write the Foreword to this book.

I am grateful to Ismael Virto, who personally knew St. Josemaría and graciously agreed to review my manuscript.

Also, my thanks go to Bert Ghezzi, my editor at OSV, who encouraged me in this project and helped it come to completion.

In my own life, the example of the men of the *Milites Ecclesiae Doctorum* have inspired me to reach for holiness as a father and husband. I am very thankful for their witness of authentic Catholic manhood.

And, of course, I deeply appreciate the patience and love of my children — Anna, Lucy, Maria, Peter, Hope, and Madeline. Their excitement about their father's work has been a great support to me.

About the Author

Eric Sammons is the author of eight books, including *Deadly Indifference* and *The Jesse Tree*. He is the editor of *Crisis Magazine*, the host of the *Crisis Point* podcast, and a former diocesan director of evangelization. He has spoken to thousands of people on various Catholic topics and has conducted evangelization, Scripture, and apologetics workshops at the parish and diocesan levels.

Sophia Institute

Sophia Institute is a nonprofit institution that seeks to nurture the spiritual, moral, and cultural life of souls and to spread the gospel of Christ in conformity with the authentic teachings of the Roman Catholic Church.

Sophia Institute Press fulfills this mission by offering translations, reprints, and new publications that afford readers a rich source of the enduring wisdom of mankind.

Sophia Institute also operates the popular online resource CatholicExchange.com. *Catholic Exchange* provides world news from a Catholic perspective as well as daily devotionals and articles that will help readers to grow in holiness and live a life consistent with the teachings of the Church.

In 2013, Sophia Institute launched Sophia Institute for Teachers to renew and rebuild Catholic culture through service to Catholic education. With the goal of nurturing the spiritual, moral, and cultural life of souls, and an abiding respect for the role and work of teachers, we strive to provide materials and programs that are at once enlightening to the mind and ennobling to the heart; faithful and complete, as well as useful and practical.

Sophia Institute gratefully recognizes the Solidarity Association for preserving and encouraging the growth of our apostolate over the course of many years. Without their generous and timely support, this book would not be in your hands.

www.SophiaInstitute.com
www.CatholicExchange.com
www.SophiaInstituteforTeachers.org

Sophia Institute Press is a registered trademark of Sophia Institute.
Sophia Institute is a tax-exempt institution as defined by the
Internal Revenue Code, Section 501(c)(3). Tax ID 22-2548708.